Editor
Lorin Klistoff, M.A.

Managing Editor
Karen Goldfluss, M.S. Ed.

Illustrator
Renée Christine Yates

Cover Artist
Barb Lorseyedi

Art Director
CJae Froshay

Art Manager
Kevin Barnes

Imaging
Rosa C. See

Publisher
Mary D. Smith, M.S. Ed.

READING, LANGUAGE & MATH ACTIVITIES
SPRING
Grades K-2

How much is the kite worth?

3¢ 3¢
2¢
3¢ 3¢

14¢

Don't "Bug" My Garden........

Author

Mary Rosenberg

Teacher Created Resources, Inc.
6421 Industry Way
Westminster, CA 92683
www.teachercreated.com

ISBN-1-4206-3890-4

©2005 Teacher Created Resources, Inc.
Made in U.S.A.

Table of Contents

Introduction

How to Use This Book

The activities in *Reading, Language & Math: Spring* are designed to grab students' interest and engage them so that they want to learn more. The activities are hands-on, fun-filled, and allow students of different academic levels to be successful. All of the activities have been kid-tested and teacher approved.

The activities can be used in a variety of ways in the primary classroom. They can be done with the whole class, in small groups, with a partner, independently, or within a designated center. Many of the activities can be sent home with the student to complete with his or her family, which reinforces the home-school connection and shows the student's family what is being taught in the classroom.

The activities in *Reading, Language & Math: Spring* also can be completed in small groups with students of differing abilities as the activities are non-competitive in nature. The activities were designed this way so that students would enjoy practicing important math or language arts skills without worrying about which person is the smartest one.

The activities are also great to use with English Language Learners. The pictures help students understand what they are supposed to do, and they help students learn vocabulary and major themes.

This book has been divided into three self-contained units. Each unit has its own table of contents, thematic activities and games, and answer key.

Writing Domains

All students need to write across the domains, in a variety of genres, and to fit specific purposes. This can be accomplished through daily writing practice and guided writing instruction. The domains are as follows:

- **Practical/Informative:** This domain can be considered reporting or "just the facts." This type of writing tells how to do something—such as writing a recipe, the steps for making a bed, or how to fill out a party invitation. (*Example:* Write the steps for giving a dog a bath.)

- **Analytical/Expository:** This domain can be considered the "convince me" form of writing. This type of writing answers "why" or "how" questions about a specific topic. The writer expresses an idea, thought, or opinion and provides supporting evidence. (*Example:* Tell why Crunchy Flakes are better than Crispy Flakes.)

- **Imaginative/Narrative:** This domain of writing is used frequently with primary age students. The writer might retell a favorite story with a new ending, tell about a familiar event, or make up a story about a favorite character. (*Example:* Pretend an eraser could talk. What would the eraser say?)

- **Sensory/Descriptive:** This domain has the student describe a certain event, object, person, or memory using words that allow the reader to create visual pictures in his or her mind. (*Example:* Describe how a hot fudge sundae tastes.)

Writing Journals

Just about anything can be used as a writing journal. Some suggestions are spiral notebooks, composition books, themed or seasonal-shaped writing paper, notepads, blank paper, lined paper, or sticky notes. You can even die-cut sheets of paper and staple the papers into individual booklets. Generic writing paper for each writing level is provided on pages 6–8.

Introduction

Sentence Frames

At the beginning of the school year, write a sentence frame on a piece of paper and photocopy it for the students. To make it easier for students to see and follow your modeling, write the sentence frame on a sentence strip or make it into an overhead transparency. As a class or a small group, complete the sentence frame. Some sample sentence frames are as follows:

- We go to _____ School.
- My name is _____.
- I live in a _____.
- My favorite color is _____.

Encourage the more capable writers to go beyond the sentence frame and write an additional sentence or two on the topic.

As students become more confident and proficient writers, sentence frames will not be needed. However, students need to see the teacher model and use good writing every day!

K-W-L Charts

K-W-L Charts are a great way to introduce a new writing topic to the students. By using a K-W-L Chart, students learn to organize information, develop questions about the topic that can serve as a guide to learning, and use the information (both previously known and newly learned) in their writing. A K-W-L Chart is provided on page 9. Make an overhead transparency of the K-W-L Chart and fill it in as a class. If desired, provided each student with a photocopy of the filled in (or partially completed) K-W-L Chart to keep in his or her writing folder.

Word Banks

Word Banks can be a rich resource for students to use when writing on a specific topic or theme. Word Banks can be written on one of the theme-related writing pages and then photocopied for the students to use, written on a chalkboard, written on an overhead, or on a seasonal-shaped piece of butcher paper. The words in the Word Bank are intended to push the student to write beyond, "I like…." If the student uses at least one of the words in the Word Bank in each sentence, the student's writing will be more interesting to read and will challenge the student to incorporate new words and phrases into his or her writing.

Two sample Word Banks are shown below. The first Word Bank contains just words. The second Word Bank uses clip art to illustrate each word. (Stickers, stamps, or drawings can also be used in place of clip art.) The illustrations make it easier for younger students to read and use the words in their writing.

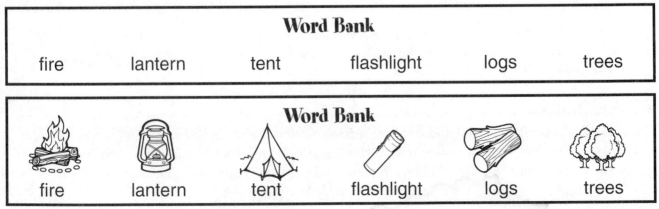

Word Bank					
fire	lantern	tent	flashlight	logs	trees

Introduction

Informal Writing Evaluation

Writing can be scored in many different ways. One way to quickly check a student's use of the mechanics of writing is to use a checklist. The checklist can include capital letters, punctuation (periods, question marks, exclamation points), spelling (usually high-frequency words and CVC words), and using sentences that answer several of the 5 W + H questions (*who, what, where, when, why,* and *how* questions). Use the blank check-off list on page 10 to help you.

Provide feedback to your students regarding their writing. Show a student an area of weakness that needs to be addressed (such as beginning each new sentence with a capital letter) and an area that has shown improvement (such as using sentences that answer some of the 5 W + H questions).

Formal Writing Evaluation

A formal rubric can be used to monitor the student's writing progress over the course of the school year. Below is a sample of a formal writing rubric.

4 Points: Exceptional Writer

- Begins each sentence with a capital letter
- Ends each sentence with a period, question mark, or exclamation point
- Capitalizes proper nouns
- Uses a variety of sentence structures to make the writing interesting to read
- Spells high-frequency words and CVC words correctly
- Takes risks in his or her writing
- Writes several sentences on the topic

3 Points: Competent Writer

- Regularly begins a sentence with a capital letter and ends each sentence with a period, question mark, or exclamation point
- Capitalizes proper nouns
- Spells many high-frequency words and CVC words correctly
- Writes more than one sentence on the topic

2 Points: Developing Writer

- Starting to begin each sentence with a capital letter
- Starting to use a period, question mark, or exclamation point at the end of the sentence
- Spells words phonetically—writing the beginning, middle, and/or ending sounds heard in the word
- Attempts to write at least one sentence on the topic
- "Reads" his or her writing to an adult

1 Point: Beginning Writer

- Writes using a string of random letters
- May or may not "read" his or her writing to an adult

_____

(Title)

_____

- -

_____

_____

- -

_____

_____

- -

_____

_____

- -

_____

- - - - - - - - - - - - - - - - - - - -

_____

K-W-L Chart

Subject: _____

What We Know	What We Would Like to Learn	What We Did Learn

Check-Off List

1.									
2.									
3.									
4.									
5.									
6.									
7.									
8.									
9.									
10.									
11.									
12.									
13.									
14.									
15.									
16.									
17.									
18.									
19.									
20.									
21.									
22.									
23.									
24.									

Leprechauns and Bunnies

Table of Contents

Introduction

This section, Leprechauns and Bunnies, contains activities that supplement events that happen in March. The bunny theme also can be used in April—depending on when Easter occurs.

Reading and Language Activities

- **St. Patrick's Day (page 15) and Easter (page 16):** Simply photocopy the pages the students are to do and use these pages as covers for these short units. Or photocopy the appropriate level of writing paper (pages 6–8) for each student and staple the cover to make a writing packet.

- **Check-Off List (page 10):** Use the blank check-off list to keep track of each student's language and reading activity as it is completed.

- **March Writing Prompts (pages 17 and 18):** Writing prompts are provided for each one of the four domains. The writing prompts are a fun way for students to explore what they know about Leprechauns and Bunnies.

- **About St. Patrick (page 19):** Students cut out the statements, sort and glue them into the appropriate category. Then students write one more true statement about St. Patrick.

- **Rabbits and Hares (page 20):** Students cut out the statements, sort and glue them into the appropriate category. Then students write one more true statement about a rabbit or a hare.

- **St. Patrick's Day (page 21):** Students place St. Patrick's Day-related vocabulary words in alphabetical order.

- **Easter Words (page 22):** Students place Easter-related vocabulary words in alphabetical order.

- **Animals that Hatch from Eggs (page 23):** Students learn about animals that hatch from eggs by doing this activity. The pages can be cut apart and then stapled to make a mini-booklet.

- **Letter Matches (pages 24–27):** These cut-and-paste activities reinforce identifying and matching uppercase and lowercase letters. Students cut out the "puzzle pieces" at the bottom of the page and glue them in place under the matching uppercase letter. If done correctly, the letters will spell a word and a picture will be revealed.

- **Making Questions and Statements (pages 28 and 29):** There are two activities, one for St. Patrick's Day and one for Easter. These activities contain rebus-like pictures and high-frequency words. Students cut apart the words and pictures and arrange and rearrange the words and pictures to make different questions and statements. When doing this activity with the whole class, make an overhead transparency of the pages or use a photocopy machine to enlarge the words and pictures so that they can be easily seen by all of the students. Some sample sentences are as follows:

Using the St. Patrick's Day Words	Using the Easter Words
Can you see the leprechaun?	The Easter Bunny has the basket.
The leprechaun sees a rainbow.	Who has the eggs?
The leprechaun loves a pot of gold.	Does the Easter Bunny have the decorated eggs?
Where is the clover?	Where are the chocolate eggs?

Introduction

Reading and Language Activities *(cont.)*

- **How Many Words Can You Make? (pages 30 and 31):** Students cut apart the letter cards and arrange and rearrange the letters to make different words. When doing this activity with the whole class, make an overhead transparency of the page. Call on individual students to use the overhead to show the class a word they have made. This is also a great activity to send home as homework. Sample words that can be made are as follows:

Using the Letters in Leprechaun	
two letters: an	*four letters:* chap, leap, earn, Earl, peel, harp
three letters: are, car, ale, pal, cap	*five or more letters:* cheap, cheep, cheer, preach
Using the Letters in Easter Bunny	
two letters: be, as, at	*four letters:* stun, ease, stab, east, star
three letters: tan, ran, bun, yet, yes, bee	*five or more letters:* stare, steer, runny, sunny

- **This Easter (pages 32 and 33):** This rebus story activity uses pictures and high-frequency words to tell a story. Students feel successful when they are able to read the story with little or no help from the teacher!

  The story reads as follows: *The Easter Bunny collected many eggs and put the eggs into the basket. The Easter Bunny went to many houses. The Easter Bunny hid the eggs behind trees, in the grass, and under the flowers. The Easter Bunny left a basket for each boy and girl. In the morning the boys and girls will look for the eggs. The boys and girls will find many eggs!*

- **Top of the Morning to You! (page 34) and Seeing Green (page 35):** Students find vocabulary words about St. Patrick's Day in a word search or a crossword puzzle.

- **In the Forest (page 36), Parts of an Egg (pages 37 and 38), and Rabbit (page 39):** In these activities, students place labels underneath a picture or write the words on a diagram. For Parts of an Egg, students also complete a word search.

- **March Bingo (pages 40–42) and Bunny Bingo (pages 43–45):** The two seasonal bingo games include eight different bingo cards and matching calling cards. The bingo games reinforce seasonal vocabulary and language development skills in a fun-filled, non-threatening manner.

- **Rhyme Time (pages 46–50):** This game introduces the concept of rhyming words in a concrete manner. The skill of rhyming can be practiced through several different games outlined on page 46. After students have had opportunities to practice rhyming, there is a follow up cut-and-paste activity provided on page 50.

- **Rabbits (page 51) and Hares (page 52):** These two pages provide students with basic information on these two topics, as well as a few questions for students to answer about what they have just read.

Math Activities

- **Finding Leprechauns (page 53) and Mystery Egg (page 54):** These are logic activities. As each clue is read, students cross off the pictures that meet (or do not meet) the clue.

- **Seeing Charms (page 55):** Students read and answer questions about a chart.

Introduction

Math Activities *(cont.)*

- **Other Lucky Charms (page 56):** Students place pictures on a graph and then answer questions about the graph.

- **Marshmallow Charms (pages 57 and 58):** Students create a graph using the marshmallow charms found in a handful of cereal. If marshmallow charms are not available, use the patterns on page 58.

- **"Eggs"actly Hours (pages 59–61):** This game can be played with a small group of students or with half the class at one time. This game reinforces reading and telling time to the hour.

- **Egg Measuring (page 62):** Students use a centimeter ruler to measure the height of different Easter eggs.

- **March Calendar (pages 63 and 64):** Students put together all the different parts of a calendar and then answer some questions about it.

- **Springtime Fun! (page 65), Luck of the Irish (page 66), and Spring Wishes (page 67):** Students glue all the pieces of the puzzle in the correct place on the graph to form a picture.

- **Where are the Eggs? (page 68):** Students identify and locate different eggs on the map.

- **Leprechaun Sorting (pages 69 and 70) and Bunny Sorting (pages 71 and 72):** These activities can be done with the whole class. Make an overhead transparency of both pages. Place the large pot of gold (or basket) on the overhead projector. Place several of the pictures inside the large shape and the remaining pictures outside the shape. Ask the students, "What is the rule to be in this family?" Call on students to answer.

  Suggested ways to sort the leprechaun pictures:

Those with bodies or just heads	Leprechauns with clovers
Those holding something	Leprechauns with belts
Leprechauns with pots of gold	

  Suggested ways to sort the bunny pictures:

Wearing clothes	Those with ties
Holding baskets	Those with bows
Those with bodies or just heads	

- **Lucky Patterns (pages 73 and 74) and Bunny Patterns (pages 75 and 76):** Students make patterns using theme-related pictures. Photocopy the pattern sleeve onto construction paper, fold and glue in the back to create the sleeve. For each student, provide three to four 12" lengths of sentence strips. Photocopy a class set of theme-related pictures. Have the students cut out the pictures and use the pictures to make different patterns on the sentence strips.

- **Find the Pot of Gold (pages 77–80):** This game has students practicing counting and adding together different combinations of pennies, nickels, and dimes.

- **St. Patrick's Day Box (page 81), Breakfast Pillow (page 82), and Bunny Box (page 83):** Three different seasonal patterns are provided. Students can create a pillow box and a small box with a St. Patrick's Day theme. Students also can make a small Easter box. Just add a small construction paper handle to turn it into a tiny Easter basket!

St. Patrick's Day

Easter

March Writing Prompts

Domain	Writing Prompt	Word Bank
Practical/Informative	Animals that Hatch from Eggs	With the students, brainstorm a list of animals that hatch from eggs.
Practical/Informative	Who Was St. Patrick?	Britain, Irish raiders, kidnapped, missionary, shepherd, wealthy parents
Practical/Informative	How to Dye an Easter Egg	boil, bowls, coloring, decorate, dye, dry, egg, spoons, stickers, tray, wax
Practical/Informative	Best Places to Hide Eggs	With the students, brainstorm a list of places where eggs can be hidden.
Analytical/Expository	Are Leprechauns Real or Imaginary?	fairies, fairy tale, imaginary, little people, pretend, real, story books
Analytical/Expository	Is the Easter Bunny Real or Imaginary?	basket, bonnet, bunny, delivering, Easter, eggs, hat, homes, hops, rabbit, tie
Analytical/Expository	Should People Be Pinched on March 17 If They Are Not Wearing Green?	With the students brainstorm a list of reasons both for and against pinching.
Analytical/Expository	Which Kind of Eggs are Better— Real Eggs or Chocolate Eggs?	chocolate, crack, delicious, eat, foil, healthy, melt, real, sweet, taste

March Writing Prompts

Domain	Writing Prompt	Word Bank
Imaginative/Narrative	What Would You Do If You Caught a Leprechaun?	family, friends, good, keep, lucky, nice, parents, pot of gold, room, share
Imaginative/Narrative	If I Found a Four Leaf Clover, I Would Wish For . . .	With the students, brainstorm a list of items and things they would wish for.
Imaginative/Narrative	What Does It Feel Like to Hatch from an Egg?	born, breathe, crack, free, out, peck, push, shove, squished, stretch
Imaginative/Narrative	Write the Easter bunny's job description.	With the students, brainstorm a list of jobs the Easter Bunny must do.
Sensory/Descriptive	Describe a leprechaun.	beard, buckles, hat, instrument, pipe, pointy ears, pointy shoes, small, tiny
Sensory/Descriptive	Describe a favorite egg.	basket, cool, delicate, decorate, eat, foil, oval-shaped, rolls, smooth, wrapped
Sensory/Descriptive	Describe a real rabbit.	big, ears, feet, furry, hop, legs, long, nibble, soft, tail, teeth, twitch, whiskers
Sensory/Descriptive	How Do You Catch a Leprechaun?	capture, forest, hold, net, pot, quiet, rainbow, run, set, sneak, tip-toe, trap

About St. Patrick

Directions: Cut out and glue each statement under the correct category.

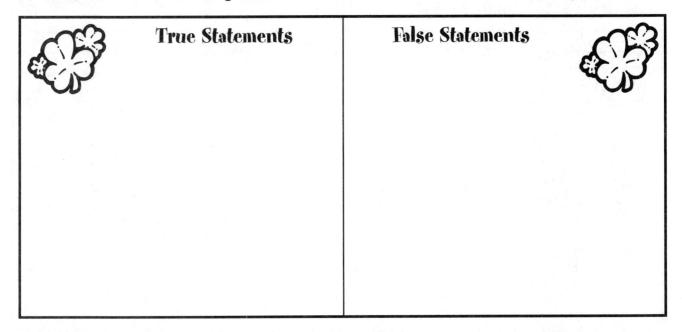

True Statements	False Statements

Directions: Write another true statement about St. Patrick.

_____

- -

_____

_____

- -

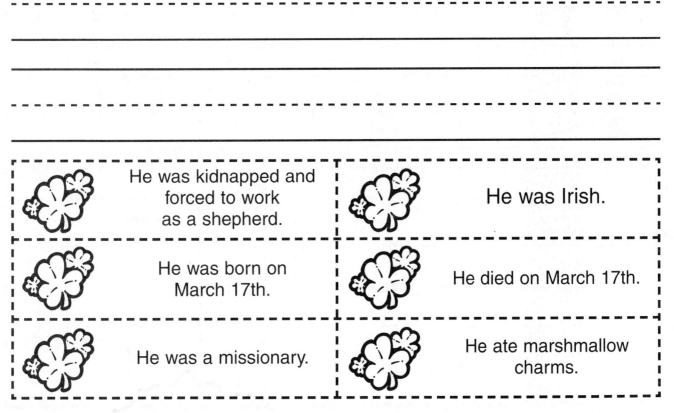

He was kidnapped and forced to work as a shepherd.	He was Irish.
He was born on March 17th.	He died on March 17th.
He was a missionary.	He ate marshmallow charms.

Rabbits and Hares

Directions: Read pages 51 and 52. Then cut out and glue each statement under the correct category.

Rabbits	Hares

Directions: Write another true statement about a rabbit or a hare.

_____

- -

_____

_____

- -

_____

born with open eyes	need to be taken care of in the nest
can hop soon after being born	born with closed eyes
born bald	born with fur

St. Patrick's Day

Directions: Cut out the words at the bottom of the page. Put the words in alphabetical order and then answer each question.

1. _____

2. _____

3. _____

4. _____

5. _____

6. Which word is <u>first</u>?

_____

7. Which word comes <u>after</u> *green*?

_____

8. Which word comes <u>before</u> *shamrock*?

_____

9. Which word is <u>last</u>?

_____

10. Which word is in <u>between</u> *leprechaun* and *pot of gold*?

_____

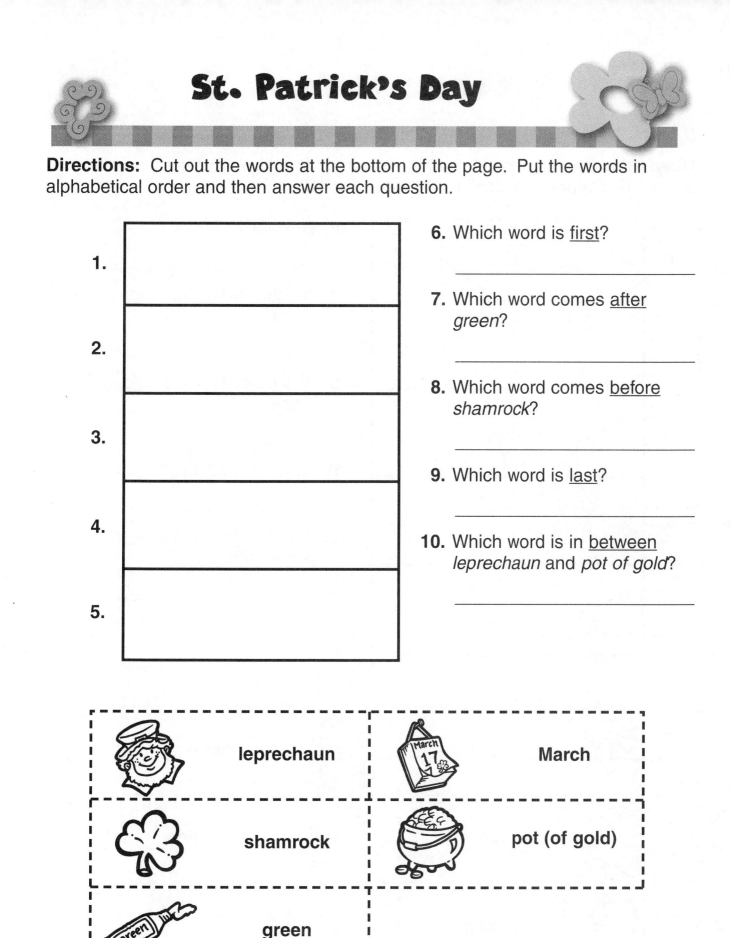

leprechaun

March

shamrock

pot (of gold)

green

Easter Words

Directions: Cut out the words at the bottom of the page. Put the words in alphabetical order and then answer each question.

1.	
2.	
3.	
4.	
5.	

6. Which word is <u>first</u>?

_____

7. Which word comes <u>after</u> *grass*?

_____

8. Which word comes <u>before</u> *rabbit*?

_____

9. Which word is <u>last</u>?

_____

10. Which word is in <u>between</u> *basket* and *grass*?

_____

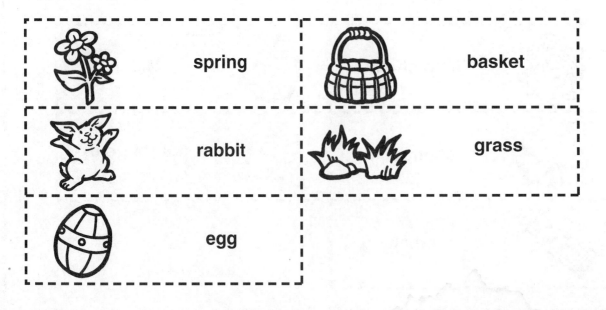

spring   basket

rabbit   grass

egg

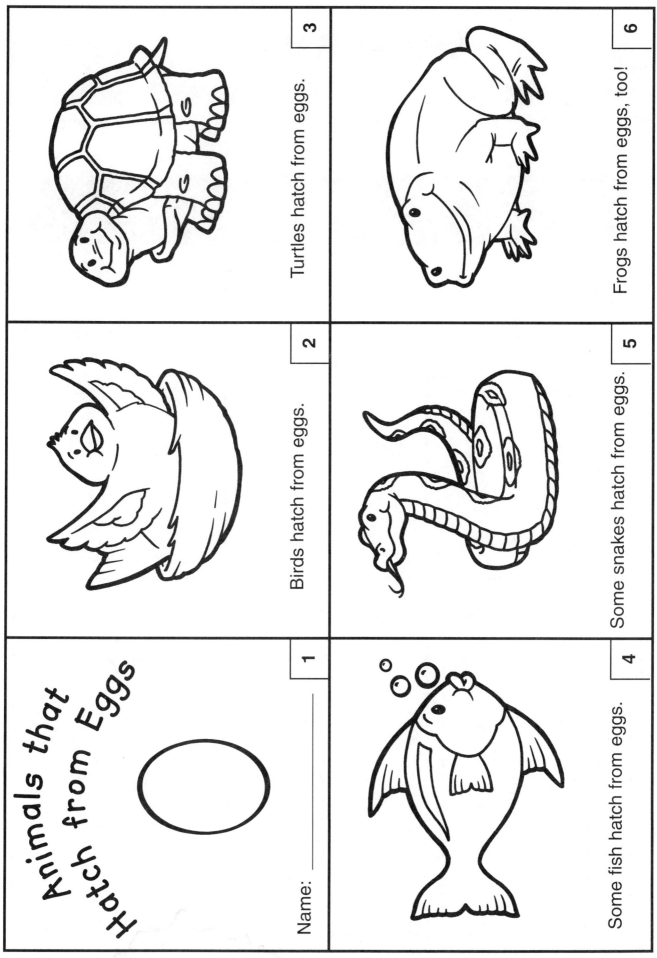

3

Turtles hatch from eggs.

6

Frogs hatch from eggs, too!

2

Birds hatch from eggs.

5

Some snakes hatch from eggs.

1

Animals that Hatch from Eggs

Name: _____

4

Some fish hatch from eggs.

Letter Match

Directions: Cut out the boxes at the bottom of the page. Glue the lowercase letter box to the uppercase letter box to find a picture.

D	Y	E

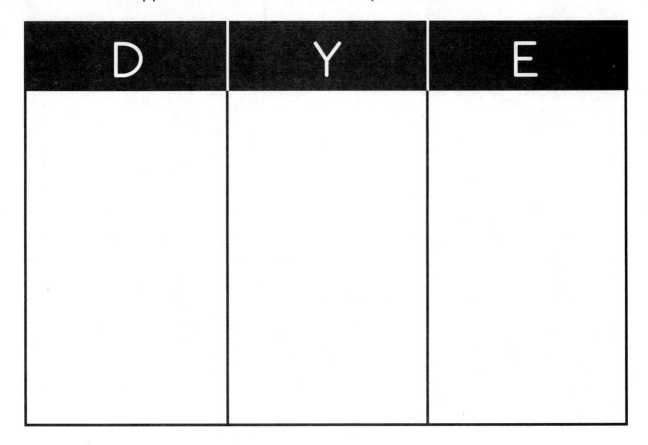

d	e	y

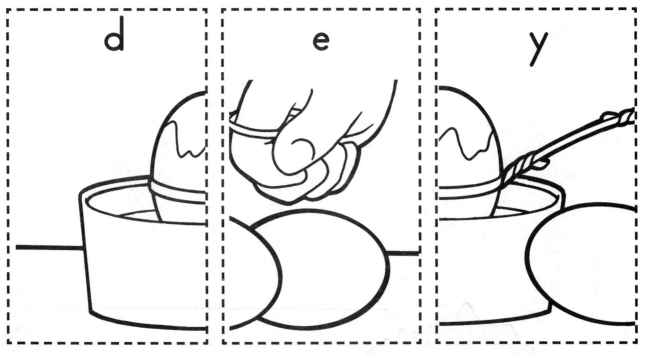

Letter Match

Directions: Cut out the boxes at the bottom of the page. Glue the lowercase letter box to the uppercase letter box to find a picture.

H	U	N	T

Letter Match

Directions: Cut out the boxes at the bottom of the page. Glue the lowercase letter box to the uppercase letter box to find a picture.

L	U	C	K	Y

c   k   l   u   y

Letter Match

Directions: Cut out the boxes at the bottom of the page. Glue the lowercase letter box to the uppercase letter box to find a picture.

B	A	S	K	E	T

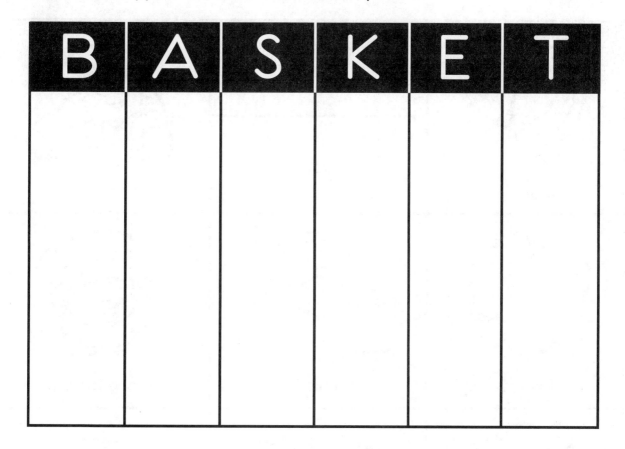

a	b	e	k	s	t

 #3890 Reading, Language & Math Activities: Spring

Making Questions and Statements

Directions: Cut apart the picture and word cards. Arrange and rearrange the cards to make different questions and statements.

lucky	I / you	see
loves	rainbow	leprechaun
clover	pot of gold	sees / the / Who
Where	a	is
has	Do	have
We	.	?

Making Questions and Statements

Directions: Cut apart the picture and word cards. Arrange and rearrange the cards to make different questions and statements.

Easter Bunny	basket	eggs
grass	bonnet	egg hunt
decorated	chocolate	Does
		the
		the
has	are	see
Where	Who	have
is	.	?

How Many Words Can You Make?

Directions: Cut out the letters at the bottom of the page. Rearrange the letters to make different words. Write each word under the correct heading.

Two-Letter Words

Three-Letter Words

Four-Letter Words

Five-or-More-Letter Words

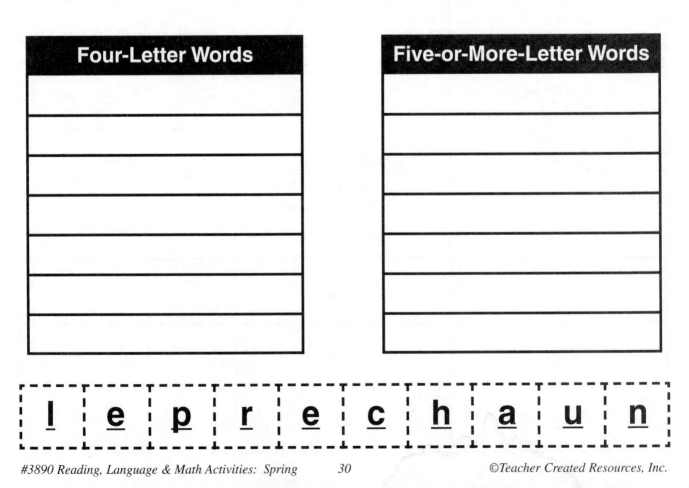

| l | e | p | r | e | c | h | a | u | n |

How Many Words Can You Make?

Directions: Cut out the letters at the bottom of the page. Rearrange the letters to make different words. Write each word under the correct heading.

Two-Letter Words

Three-Letter Words

Four-Letter Words

Five-or-More-Letter Words

E a s t e r B u n n y

This Easter

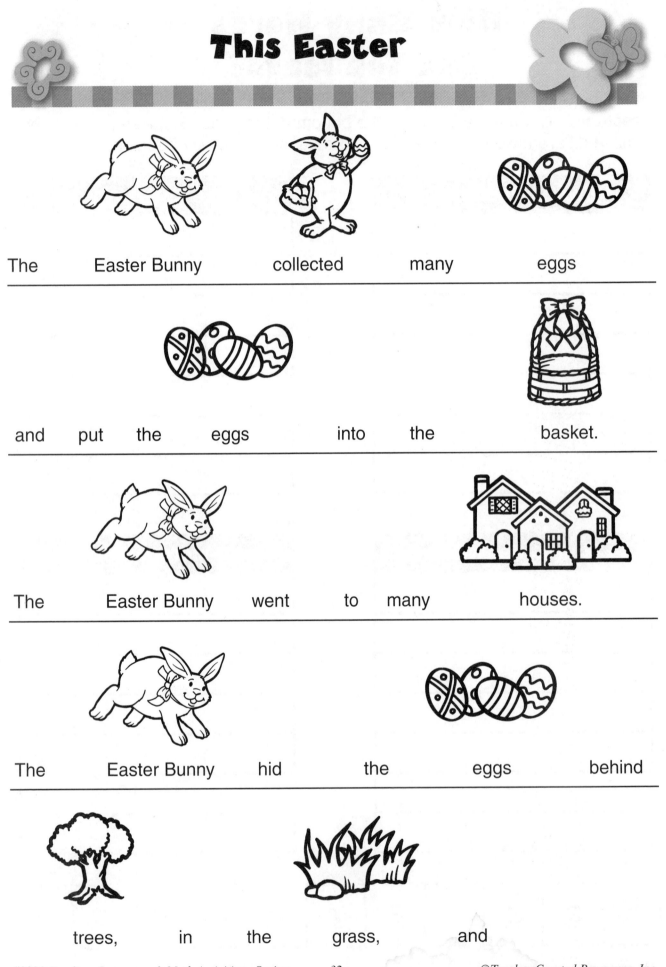

The   Easter Bunny   collected   many   eggs

and   put   the   eggs   into   the   basket.

The   Easter Bunny   went   to   many   houses.

The   Easter Bunny   hid   the   eggs   behind

trees,   in   the   grass,   and

This Easter

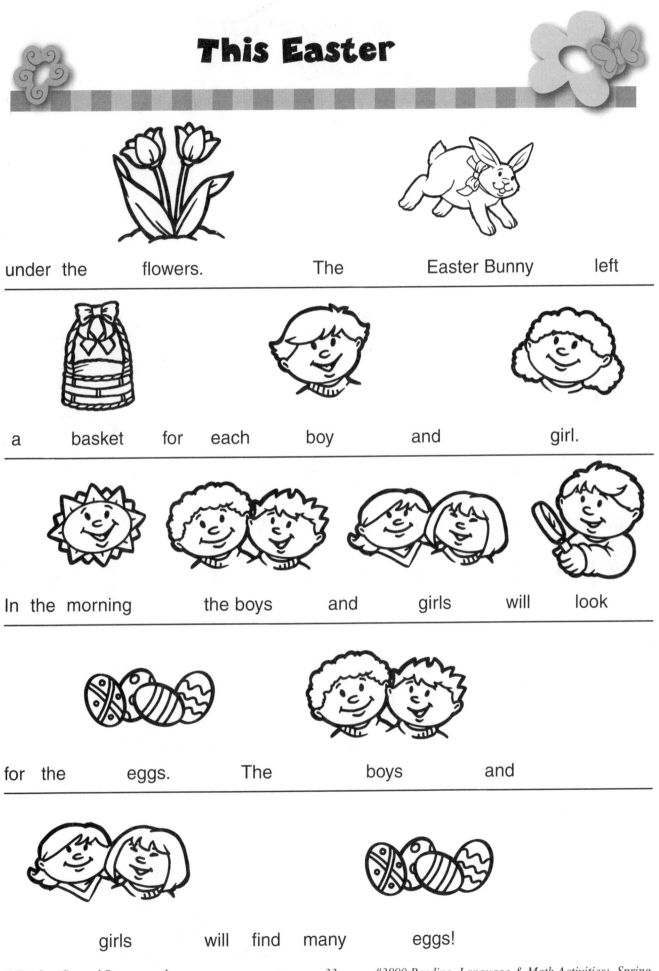

under the   flowers.   The   Easter Bunny   left

a   basket   for   each   boy   and   girl.

In the morning   the boys   and   girls   will   look

for   the   eggs.   The   boys   and

girls   will   find   many   eggs!

Top of the Morning to You!

Directions: Find and color each word.

```
H  O  R  S  E  S  H  O  E  A  B  S
A  A  R  Z  Y  T  K  X  V  S  H  T
B  R  J  I  R  E  L  A  N  D  G  P
Q  A  I  I  J  U  H  H  Q  T  O  A
F  I  R  L  S  T  P  O  T  G  L  T
Q  N  S  U  F  K  I  W  P  P  D  R
P  B  C  C  C  B  C  O  I  N  S  I
M  O  O  K  L  E  K  V  E  L  D  C
Y  W  Z  Y  S  H  A  M  R  O  C  K
M  D  O  G  R  E  E  N  F  O  N  E
H  M  A  R  C  H  N  U  W  M  C  N
L  E  P  R  E  C  H  A  U  N  X  G
```

COINS	IRELAND	POT
GOLD	LEPRECHAUN	RAINBOW
GREEN	LUCKY	SHAMROCK
HORSESHOE	MARCH	ST. PATRICK

Seeing Green

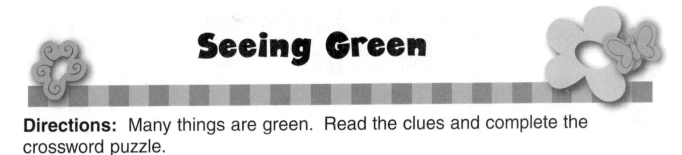

Directions: Many things are green. Read the clues and complete the crossword puzzle.

APPLES   BEANS   EGGS   EMERALD   EYES

GRASS   LIGHT   PLANT   TEA   THUMB

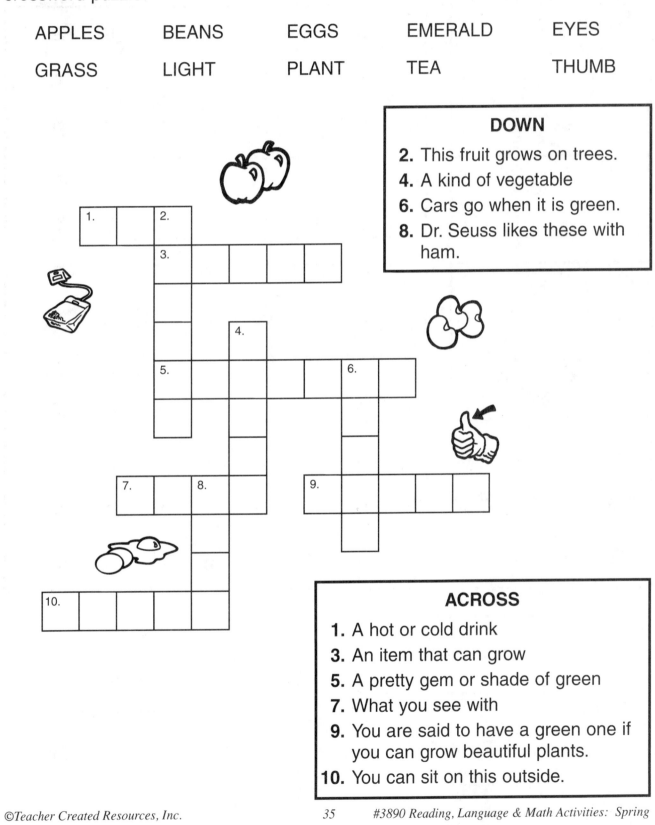

DOWN

2. This fruit grows on trees.

4. A kind of vegetable

6. Cars go when it is green.

8. Dr. Seuss likes these with ham.

ACROSS

1. A hot or cold drink

3. An item that can grow

5. A pretty gem or shade of green

7. What you see with

9. You are said to have a green one if you can grow beautiful plants.

10. You can sit on this outside.

In the Forest

Directions: Cut out and glue each word under the correct picture.

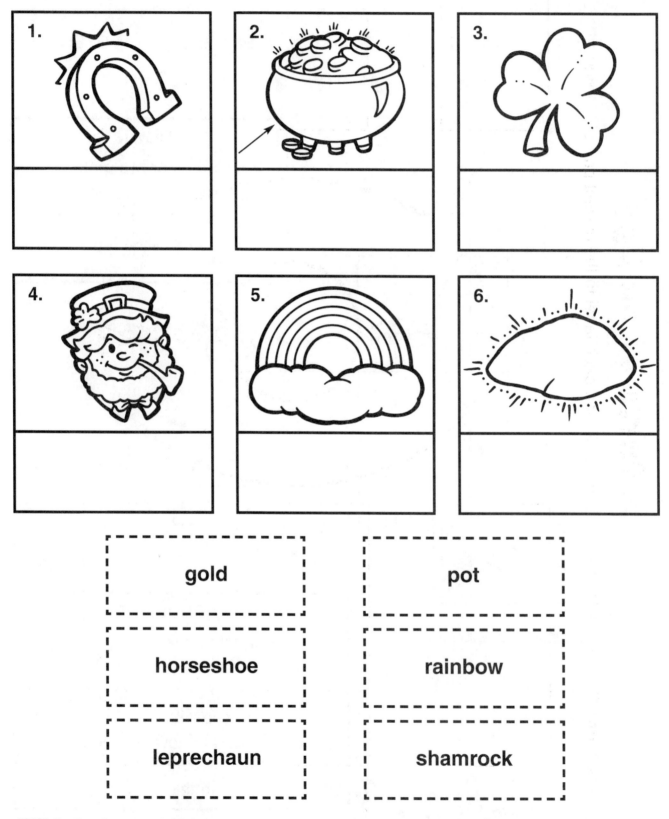

Parts of an Egg

Directions: Cut out the labels on page 38. Match each label to the correct part of the egg.

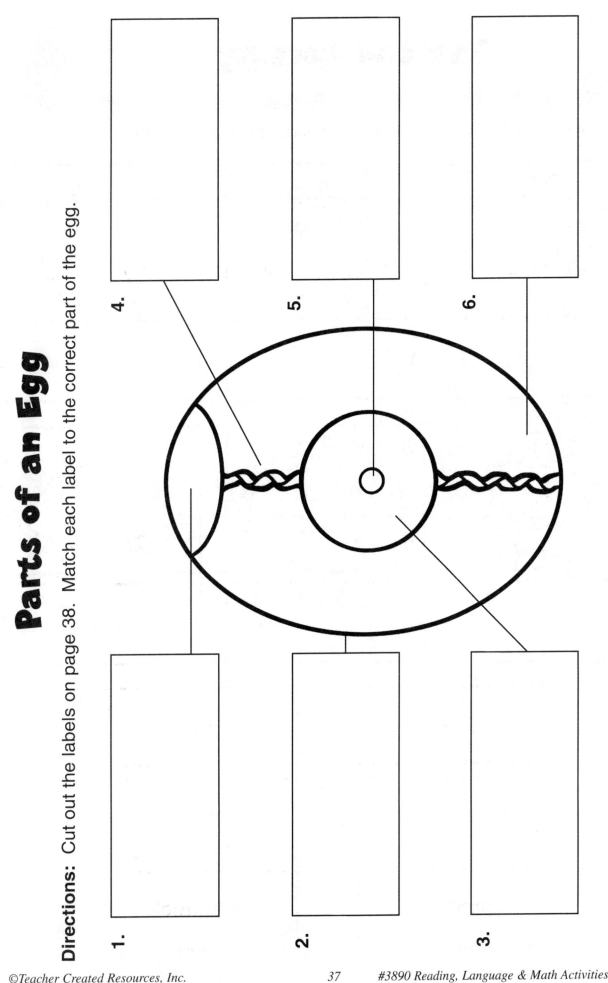

1.

2.

3.

4.

5.

6.

Parts of an Egg

Directions: Find and color each word in the word search.

AIR CELL   ALBUMEN   CHALAZA   EMBRYO   SHELL   YOLK

A	A	L	S	F	L	M	T	F	O	G	Y
I	K	X	K	J	W	E	F	V	U	U	O
R	E	E	C	H	A	L	A	Z	A	T	L
C	Y	M	Z	V	I	E	Z	B	N	S	K
E	K	B	A	L	B	U	M	E	N	D	P
L	R	R	A	Q	A	M	Y	G	X	D	C
L	P	Y	J	D	B	N	B	R	C	W	H
Q	C	O	O	H	V	I	S	H	E	L	L

Directions: Cut out the boxes and glue them in the correct places on page 37.

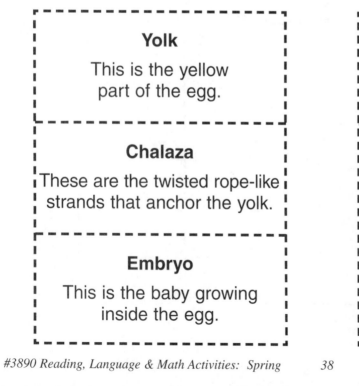

Yolk

This is the yellow
part of the egg.

Chalaza

These are the twisted rope-like
strands that anchor the yolk.

Embryo

This is the baby growing
inside the egg.

Albumen

This is the egg white.
It is nearest to the shell.

Air Cell

This is the pocket of air
at the large end of the egg.

Shell

This is the outer part of the
egg. It helps protect the baby.

Rabbit

Directions: Label each part of the rabbit.

body	ear	leg	nose	tail	whiskers

1.

2.

3.

4.

5.

6.

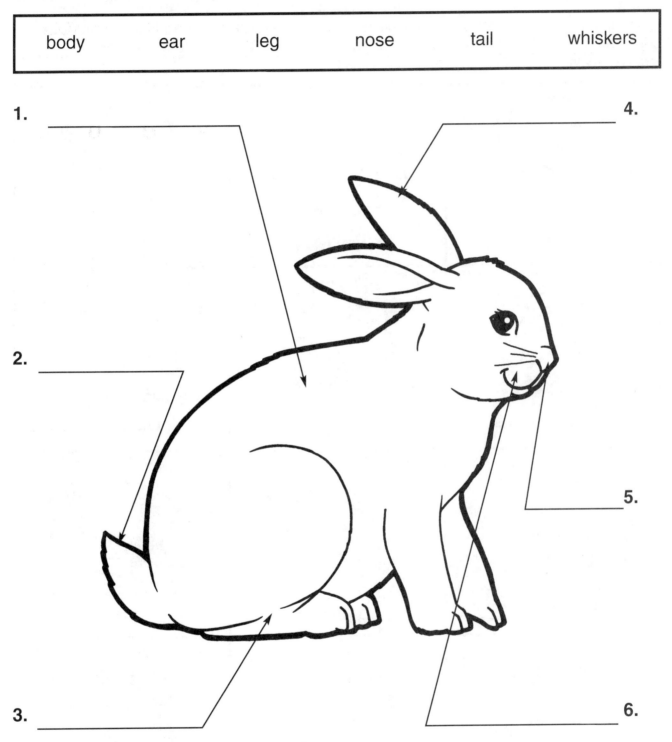

March Bingo

Directions: Photocopy the calling cards below onto cardstock, color, laminate, and cut apart. Provide each student with a game board (pages 41 and 42) and some counters (beans, pennies, multilinks, etc.). Mix up the calling cards. As each card is read aloud, have students cover the matching picture on their boards with a counter. The first student to get three in a row (vertically, horizontally, or diagonally) wins the game.

leprechaun	rainbow	gold
horseshoe	shamrock	Ireland
March 17	green	hat
saint	forest	castle

March Bingo

Card 1

March Bingo

gold	forest	leprechaun
rainbow	Free Space	saint
horseshoe	March 17	hat

Card 2

March Bingo

rainbow	leprechaun	shamrock
Ireland	Free Space	forest
green	gold	castle

Card 3

March Bingo

leprechaun	gold	hat
green	Free Space	Ireland
forest	horseshoe	saint

Card 4

March Bingo

castle	saint	horseshoe
shamrock	Free Space	forest
leprechaun	gold	March 17

March Bingo

Card 5

March Bingo

castle	Ireland	forest
horseshoe	Free Space	green
shamrock	rainbow	March 17

Card 6

March Bingo

gold	castle	horseshoe
rainbow	Free Space	leprechaun
saint	shamrock	hat

Card 7

March Bingo

March 17	hat	castle
forest	Free Space	leprechaun
gold	Ireland	shamrock

Card 8

March Bingo

gold	castle	Ireland
forest	Free Space	shamrock
green	March 17	saint

Bunny Bingo

Directions: Photocopy the calling cards below onto cardstock, color, laminate, and cut apart. Provide each student with a game board (pages 44 and 45) and some counters (beans, pennies, multilinks, etc.). Mix up the calling cards. As each card is read aloud, have students cover the matching picture on their boards with a counter. The first student to get three in a row (vertically, horizontally, or diagonally) wins the game.

basket	bonnet	rabbit
chick	decorated	grass
egg	chocolate	jelly beans
dye	hide	find

Bunny Bingo

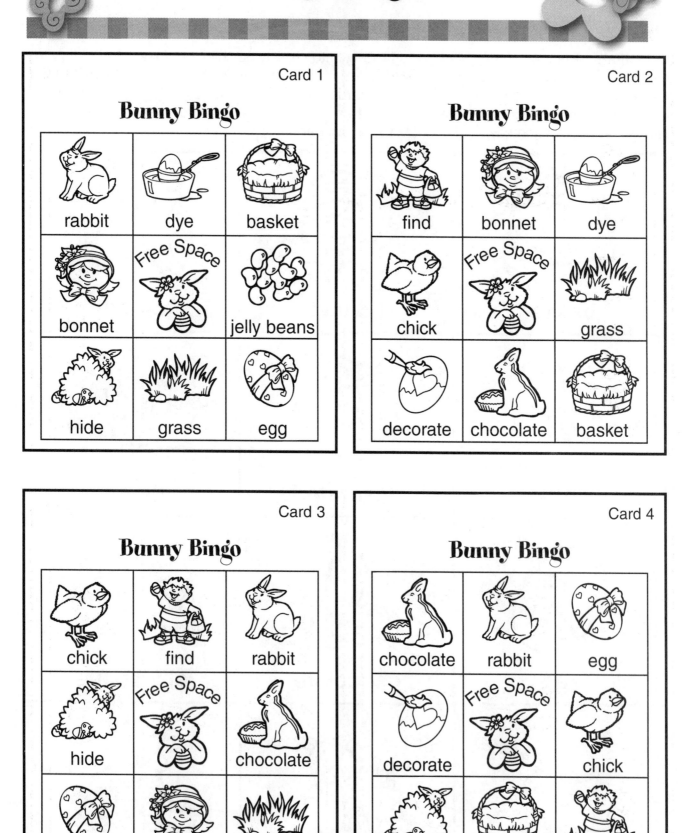

Card 1

Bunny Bingo

rabbit	dye	basket
bonnet	Free Space	jelly beans
hide	grass	egg

Card 2

Bunny Bingo

find	bonnet	dye
chick	Free Space	grass
decorate	chocolate	basket

Card 3

Bunny Bingo

chick	find	rabbit
hide	Free Space	chocolate
egg	bonnet	grass

Card 4

Bunny Bingo

chocolate	rabbit	egg
decorate	Free Space	chick
hide	basket	find

Bunny Bingo

Card 5

Bunny Bingo

hide	basket	chocolate
rabbit	Free Space	chick
jelly beans	decorate	grass

Card 6

Bunny Bingo

decorate	dye	bonnet
egg	Free Space	chocolate
decorate	rabbit	jelly beans

Card 7

Bunny Bingo

grass	dye	chick
basket	Free Space	decorate
bonnet	find	jelly beans

Card 8

Bunny Bingo

basket	hide	egg
jelly beans	Free Space	bonnet
rabbit	dye	chick

Rhyme Time

Rhyme Time uses picture cards and words as a way to introduce and practice the concept of rhyming words.

Directions

1. Photocopy the cards (pages 47–49) onto cardstock, color, laminate, and cut out.

2. Review the cards with the students.

3. Tell the students that rhyming words are words that have the same ending sound, like *cat* and *hat*. Both *cat* and *hat* end in the *–at* sound. Remind students that some rhyming words have the same ending sound but that ending sound is spelled differently like *bead* and *seed*.

4. Lay the cards out on the table and ask a student to find two cards that rhyme. Have the student name the two rhyming words. Repeat this step until all of the cards are matched.

5. Complete the cut-and-paste activity sheet on page 50.

6. As an extension idea, challenge students to name another word or words that rhyme with a specific card. (Example: *egg*, *leg*, *beg*, and *peg*)

Play Concentration

1. Using two sets of the cards, shuffle the cards together, and lay them face down on the table.

2. Taking turns, each student turns over two cards. If the words rhyme, the student keeps both cards and takes another turn. If the words do not rhyme, the student turns both cards back over and play continues with the next student.

Play "Go Rhyme" (AKA "Go Fish")

1. Make several sets of the cards. Deal out five cards to each student. Place the remaining cards in a stack, facedown on the table. Have each student remove any pairs of rhyming words that he or she is holding.

2. Taking turns, the first student asks the player on his or her left, "Do you have a word that rhymes with *(rhyming word that the student is currently holding)*?" If the player has the card, he or she hands it to the student. If the player does not have the card, he or she tells the student to "Go rhyme" (take a card from the remaining stack of cards).

3. The winner will be either the player who makes the most pairs of rhyming words or the first player to run out of cards.

Rhyme Time

egg

leg

bunny

punt

money

hunt

Rhyme Time

dye

cry

bride

grass

hide

class

Rhyme Time

roll

bowl

sick

clothes

chick

bows

Rhyme Time

Directions: Cut out and match the rhyming pictures.

1. egg

2. clothes

3. hunt

4. bunny

5. tree

6. dye

7. roll

8. chick

leg

see

punt

cry

bowl

money

toes

sick

Rabbits

Directions: Read the information in the box and answer the questions below.

Rabbits are mammals. There are 25 different kinds of rabbits. Rabbits have big ears, short tails, and strong back legs. Rabbits grow to be about 1–2 feet long. Rabbits use their legs for hopping and digging. Rabbits also have good hearing.

Rabbits are born blind and without any fur. The mother rabbit takes care of the babies in a nest.

Rabbits are herbivores. Herbivores are plant eaters. Rabbits eat grasses, leaves, bark, and twigs.

Rabbits can live just about anywhere except for Antarctica.

1. What kind of animals are rabbits?

birds ○   reptiles ○   mammals ○

2. What do herbivores eat?

plants ○   meat ○   eggs ○

3. Where do rabbits <u>not</u> live?

deserts ○   Antarctica ○   forests ○

4. What do rabbits use their strong hind (back) legs for?

climbing ○   sleeping ○   digging ○

Hares

Directions: Read the information in the box and answer the questions below.

Hares are related to rabbits. Hares are mammals. They have long ears and strong back legs. Hares hop like a kangaroo. Hares grow to be about 1-2 feet long and weigh between 3–12 pounds. Their tails are 2–4 inches long.

Hares are born with their eyes open and with fur on their bodies. Soon after being born, hares are able to hop.

A hare's fur changes color with the seasons. This is known as **camouflage.** A hare's fur may be brown, tan, reddish, gray, or white.

Hares are herbivores. That means they eat plants.

1. What happens to a hare's fur?

becomes curly ◯   grows long ◯   changes color ◯

2. How is a hare like a rabbit?

both have long ears ◯   both born with open eyes ◯   both born with fur ◯

3. What animal does a hare hop like?

cricket ◯   frog ◯   kangaroo ◯

4. What can a hare do soon after being born?

talk ◯   hop ◯   drive ◯

Finding Leprechauns

Directions: Read each clue. If the answer is "yes" make an **O** in the box. If the answer is "no" make an **X** in the box. The fill in the answers below.

	Castle	Forest	Rainbow	Mushroom
Liza				
Paula				
Rick				
Will				

CLUES

- Paula found a leprechaun by a plant.
- Rick found a leprechaun at the end of the rainbow.
- Liza found a leprechaun while walking through the forest.

1. Liza found a leprechaun in the _____.

 2. Rick found a leprechaun by a _____.

 3. Paula found a leprechaun by a _____.

 4. Will found a leprechaun by a _____.

Mystery Egg

Directions: Which egg is filled with chocolate? Read the clues and cross off the pictures that do not fit the clues.

CLUES

- The egg is decorated.
- It is by itself.
- It has more than three hearts on it.

Which egg is filled with chocolate? _____

Directions: Write another clue that would fit the mystery egg.

_____

- -

_____

Seeing Charms

Directions: Answer the questions about the chart.

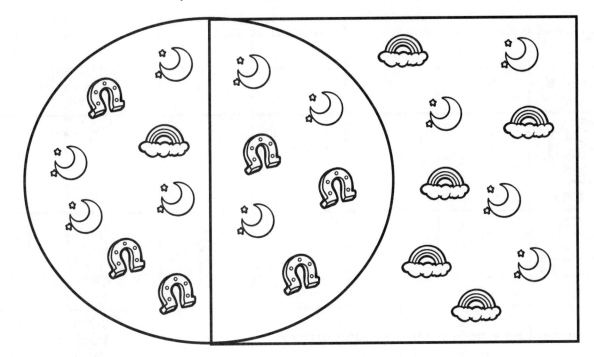

1. How many of each item are shown on the chart?

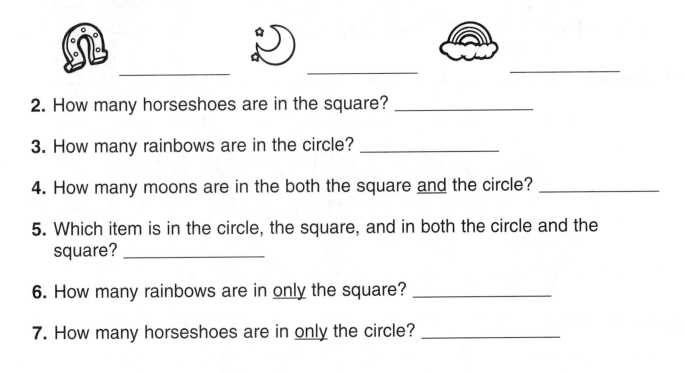

_____   _____   _____

2. How many horseshoes are in the square? _____

3. How many rainbows are in the circle? _____

4. How many moons are in the both the square <u>and</u> the circle? _____

5. Which item is in the circle, the square, and in both the circle and the square? _____

6. How many rainbows are in <u>only</u> the square? _____

7. How many horseshoes are in <u>only</u> the circle? _____

Other Lucky Charms

Directions: Use the pictures to create a graph. Answer the questions.

Rabbit's Foot						
Penny						
2 Number						

1. Which lucky item do most kids carry?

2. Do fewer kids carry 🪙 or **2** for a lucky item?

3. Do more kids carry 🐾 or **2** for a lucky item?

4. Which lucky item would you like to have?

Marshmallow Charms

Directions: Color one space for each kind of marshmallow.

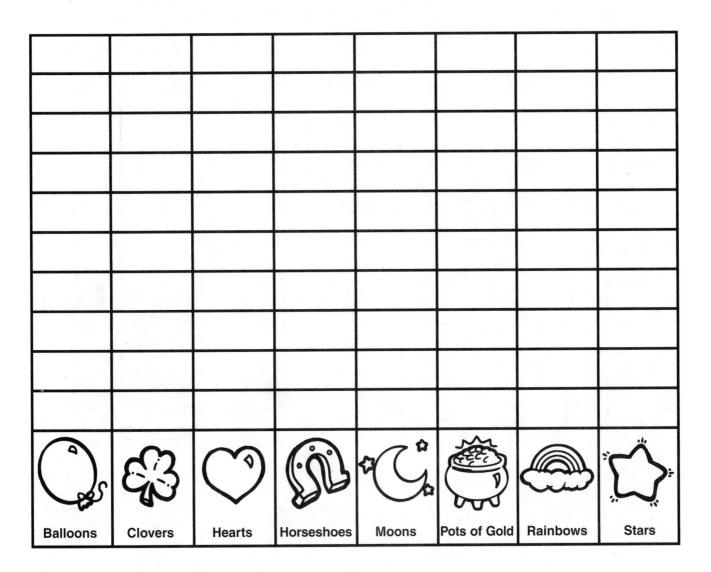

| Balloons | Clovers | Hearts | Horseshoes | Moons | Pots of Gold | Rainbows | Stars |

1. Which marshmallow shape were there the most of? _____
2. Which marshmallow shape were there the fewest of? _____
3. Which shapes had the same number of marshmallows? _____

Complete the math problems.

4. Stars + Rainbows: _____ + _____ = _____
5. Moons – Pots of Gold: _____ – _____ = _____
6. Horseshoes + Balloons: _____ + _____ = _____
7. Which two marshmallow shapes when added together equal 10?

   _____   _____

Marshmallow Charms

Directions: Use these pictures with the activity on page 57.

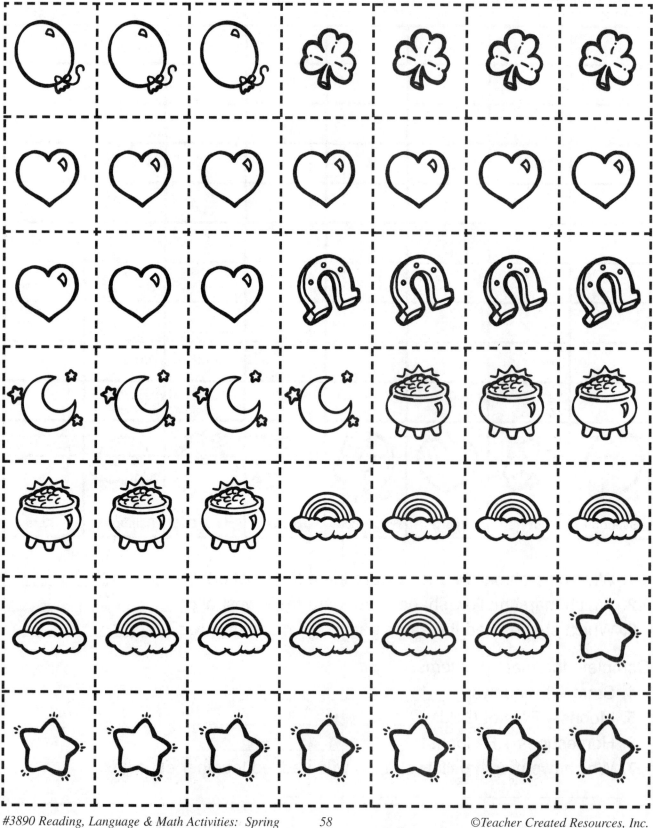

"Eggs"actly Hours

Directions: Photocopy the cards (pages 59–61) onto cardstock or construction paper and cut apart. Give each student a card. Select a student to read the sentence and identify the time at the top of the card and then read the information at the bottom of the card. The student with the matching time showing on his or her egg clock then reads his or her card. Play continues until the time needed returns to the first player.

My time is

I am looking for the egg
with the time of

11:00

My time is

I am looking for the egg
with the time of

4:00

My time is

I am looking for the egg
with the time of

6:00

My time is

I am looking for the egg
with the time of

9:00

My time is

I am looking for the egg
with the time of

2:00

My time is

I am looking for the egg
with the time of

1:00

My time is

I am looking for the egg
with the time of

12:00

My time is

I am looking for the egg
with the time of

10:00

"Eggs"actly Hours

My time is

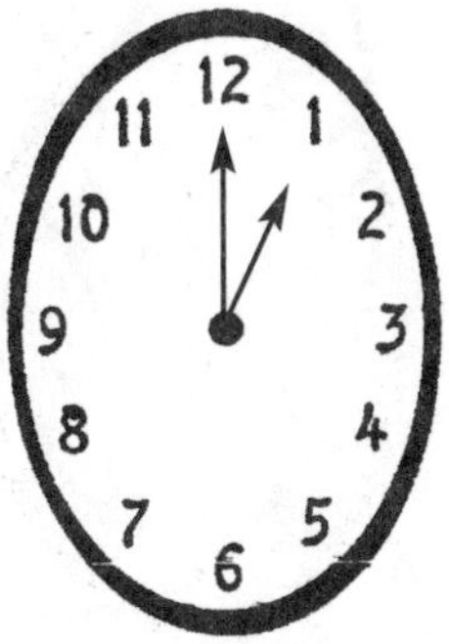

My time is

I am looking for the egg
with the time of

3:00

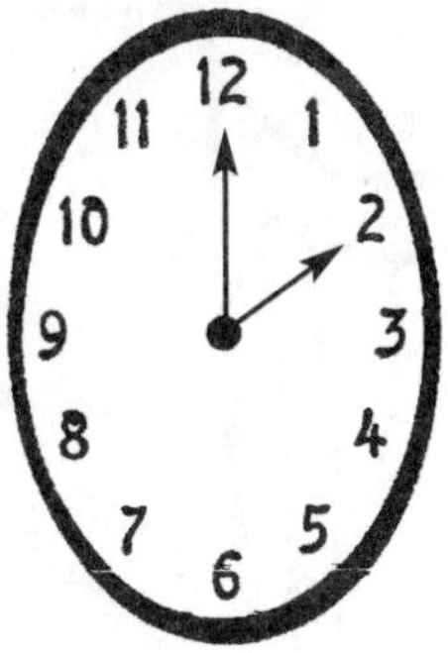

I am looking for the egg
with the time of

8:00

My time is

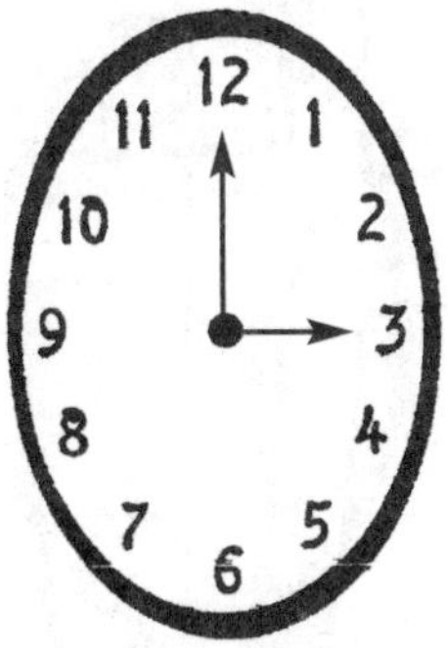

My time is

I am looking for the egg
with the time of

5:00

I am looking for the egg
with the time of

7:00

Egg Measuring

Directions: Cut out the centimeter ruler. Use the ruler to measure the height of each egg to the nearest centimeter (cm).

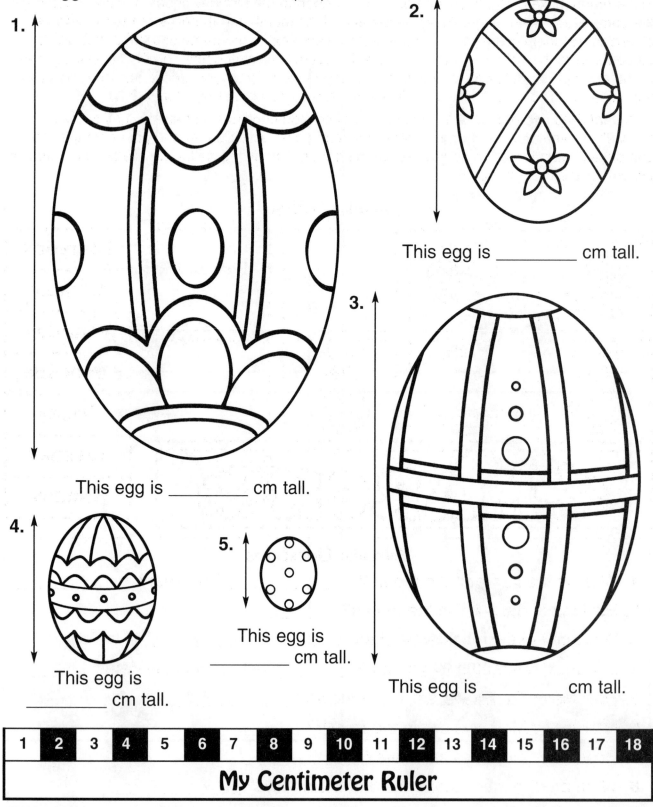

1.

2.

This egg is _____ cm tall.

3.

This egg is _____ cm tall.

4.

This egg is _____ cm tall.

5.

This egg is _____ cm tall.

This egg is _____ cm tall.

This egg is _____ cm tall.

1	2	3	4	5	6	7	8	9	10	11	12	13	14	15	16	17	18

My Centimeter Ruler

March Calendar

Directions: Photocopy the blank calendar (page 64) and the calendar "fill-ins" on this page. Make a clean copy of the calendar fill-in page first and add any special school or local events in the empty boxes. Students' names can be added to the birthday squares. Then photocopy the completed "fill-in" page. Have students add the month and the days of the week to the calendar. (Students also can write the current year next to the name of the month.) Have students write the calendar numbers in each square. Have students add the special squares to the appropriate dates on the calendar. Using markers or crayons, have the students color the calendar. Then have students answer the questions about the calendars.

(*Optional Step:* Fold a 12" x 18" inch piece of colored construction paper in half to make it 12" x 9". Have students open the folded piece of construction paper and glue or staple the completed calendar to the bottom half of the paper. On the top half, have the students draw a picture for the current month.)

Calendar "Fill-Ins"

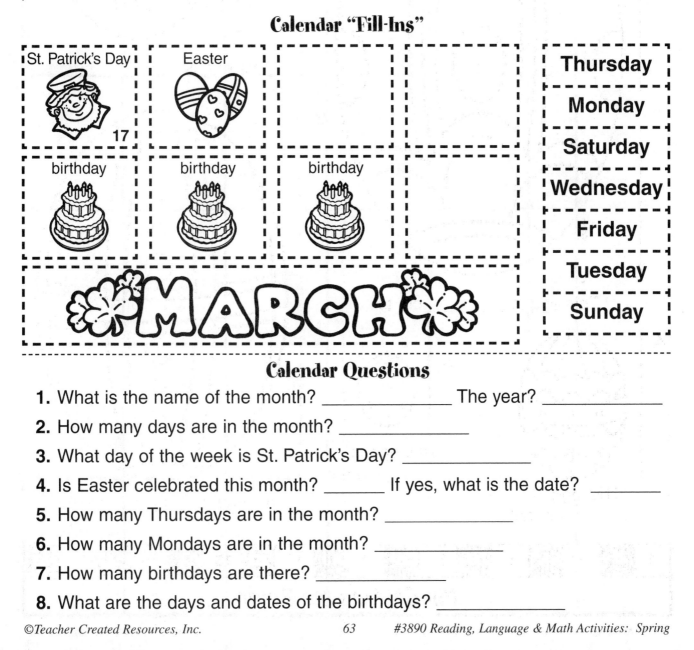

Calendar Questions

1. What is the name of the month? _____ The year? _____

2. How many days are in the month? _____

3. What day of the week is St. Patrick's Day? _____

4. Is Easter celebrated this month? _____ If yes, what is the date? _____

5. How many Thursdays are in the month? _____

6. How many Mondays are in the month? _____

7. How many birthdays are there? _____

8. What are the days and dates of the birthdays? _____

Springtime Fun!

Directions: Cut out the puzzle pieces at the bottom of the page. Glue each puzzle piece in the correct space.

	1	2	3
A			
B			

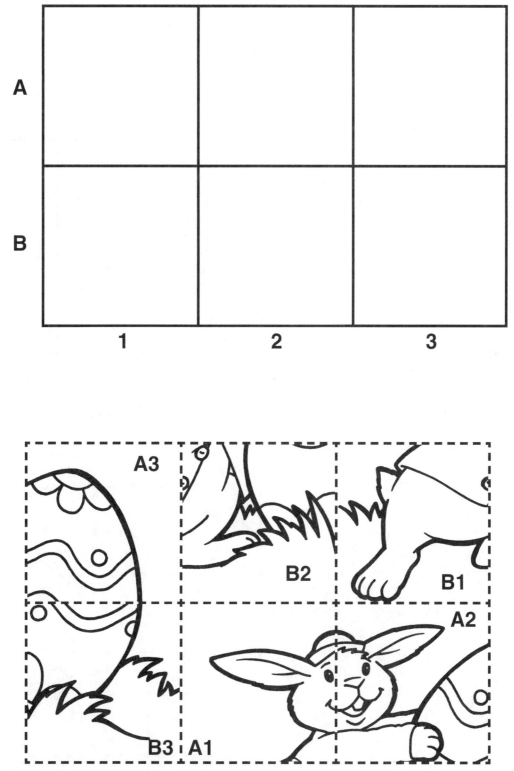

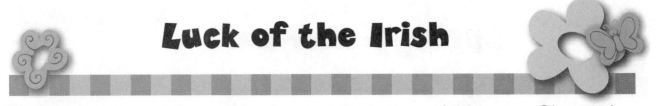

Luck of the Irish

Directions: Cut out the puzzle pieces at the bottom of the page. Glue each puzzle piece in the correct space.

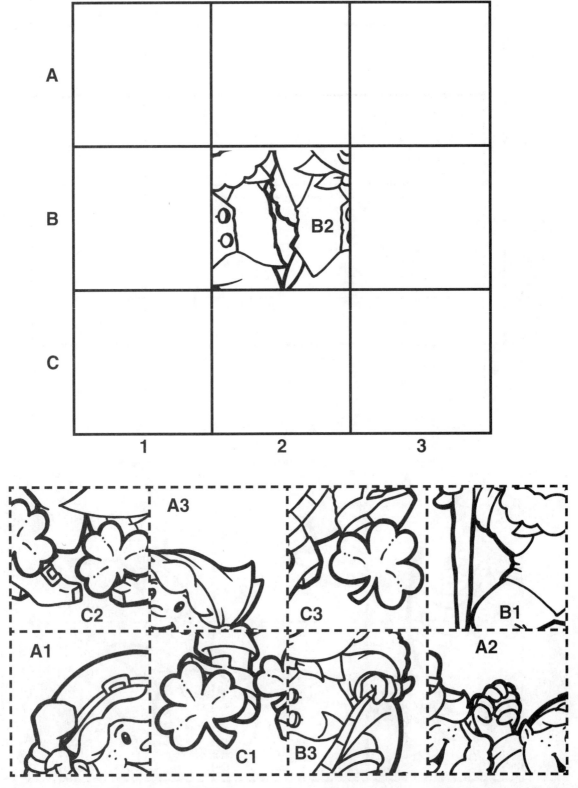

Spring Wishes

Directions: Cut out the puzzle pieces at the bottom of the page. Glue each puzzle piece in the correct space.

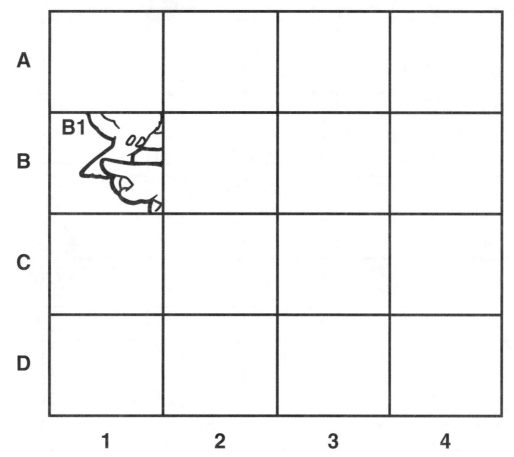

	1	2	3	4
A				
B	B1			
C				
D				

Where are the Eggs?

Directions: Use the map to answer the questions.

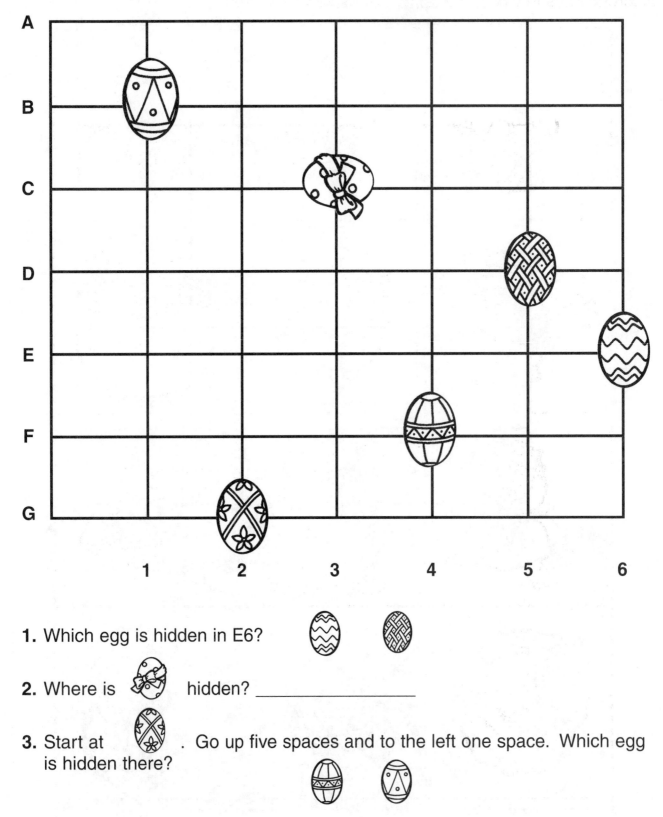

1. Which egg is hidden in E6?

2. Where is 🥚 hidden? _____

3. Start at 🥚. Go up five spaces and to the left one space. Which egg is hidden there?

Leprechaun Sorting

Directions: Cut out the leprechaun pictures. Use the pot (page 70) to find the different ways in which the leprechauns can be sorted.

Leprechaun Sorting

Directions: Put the leprechauns (page 69) that have something in common into the pot of gold.

To be in this family _____.

Bunny Sorting

Directions: Cut out the bunny pictures. Use the basket mat (page 72) to find the different ways the bunnies can be sorted.

Bunny Sorting

Directions: Put the bunnies (page 71) that have something in common into the basket.

To be in this family _____.

Lucky Patterns

Directions: Photocopy a class set of this page onto white construction paper. Have students color and cut out the squares and arrange the squares in different patterns. Glue the squares onto a 12" long sentence strip. (*Optional:* Use the pattern sleeve on page 74.)

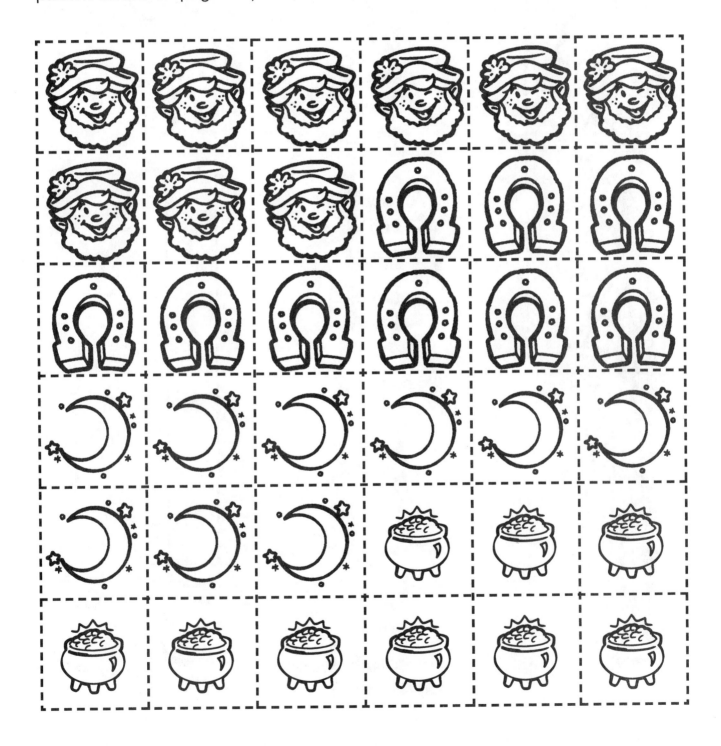

Lucky Patterns

Name: _____

Glue here.

Glue here.

Glue here.

74

Bunny Patterns

Directions: Photocopy a class set of this page onto white construction paper. Have students color and cut out the squares and arrange the squares in different patterns. Glue the squares onto a 12" long sentence strip. (*Optional:* Use the pattern sleeve on page 76.)

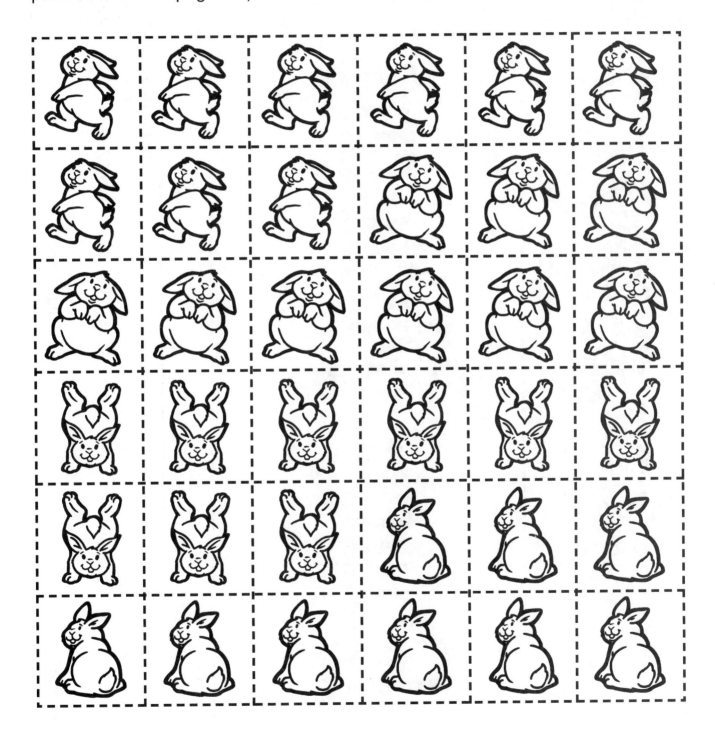

Bunny Patterns

Name: _____

Find the Pot of Gold

Directions: This is a money game for two to four players. For each small group of students, provide a game board, a set of playing cards, and a set of tokens. Each student places his or her token in the start box. Taking turns, each player turns over a card, counts the money, and moves his or her token to the nearest matching square. If a student lands in a space to the left of the rainbow, he or she may slide across the rainbow and land in the other square. The rainbow is a short cut. If a student lands in a space already occupied by another player, the first player is bumped back to start. To win, the student must land in the square right next to the pot of gold.

Find the Pot of Gold

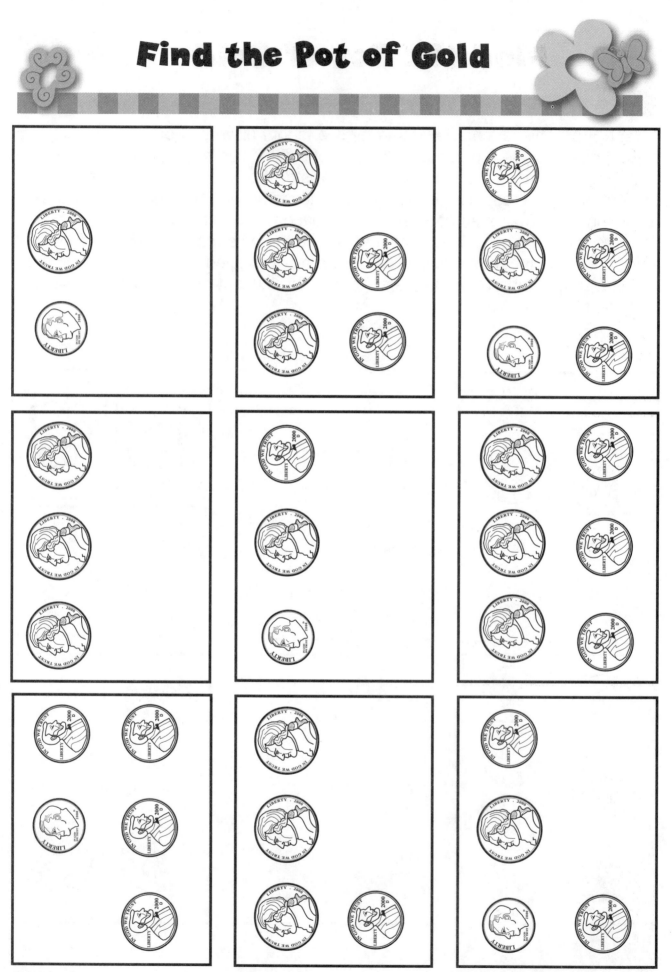

78

Find the Pot of Gold

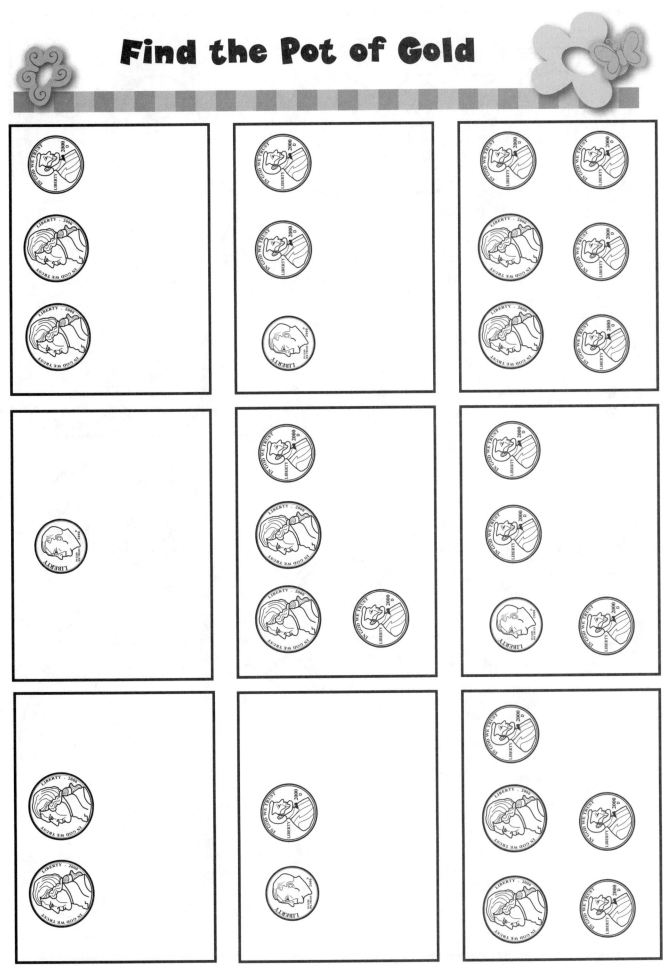

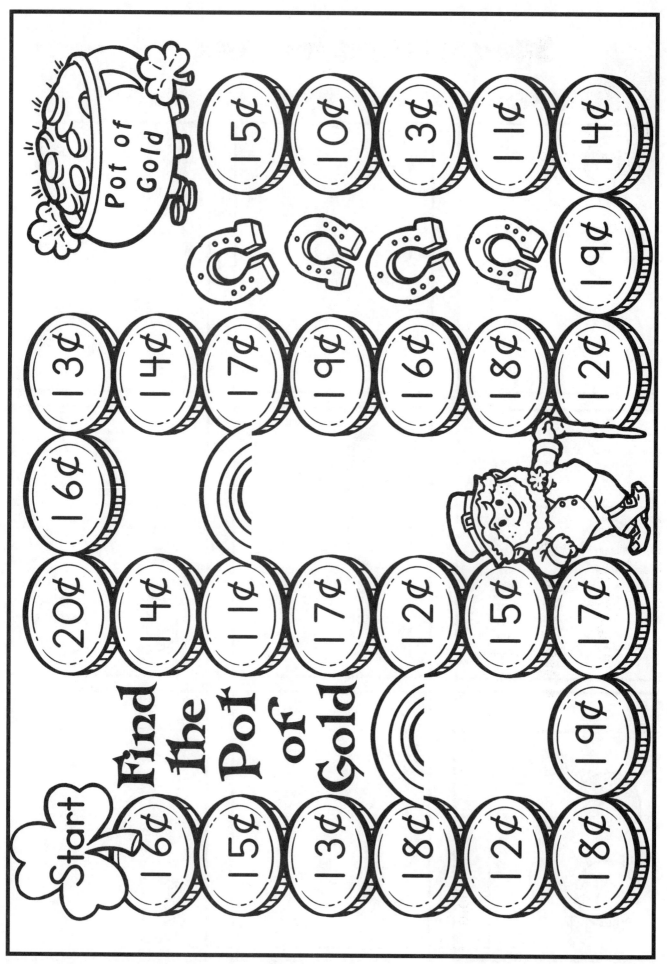

Pot of Gold

15¢ 10¢ 3¢ 1¢ 4¢

9¢

3¢ 4¢ 7¢ 9¢ 6¢ 8¢ 2¢

16¢

20¢ 4¢ 1¢ 7¢ 2¢ 5¢ 7¢

Find the Pot of Gold

19¢

Start 6¢ 5¢ 3¢ 8¢ 2¢ 8¢

St. Patrick's Day Box

Directions

1. Color the pictures.
2. Cut on the solid lines.
3. Fold on the dashed lines.
4. Put glue or tape on the tabs and fold and attach to the neighboring side.

Breakfast Pillow

Directions: Color the picture. Cut on the thick solid lines. Use the pointy end of the pen cap to score (press really hard) on the dashed lines. Put glue or tape on the end and attach it to the other side of the pattern. Push in the oval sections at one end of the pillow and fill with cereal. Push in the oval sections at the other end to close the pillow box.

Top of the Morning to you!

Put glue or tape here.

Bunny Box

Directions

1. Color the pictures.
2. Cut on the solid lines.
3. Fold on the dashed lines.
4. Put glue or tape on the tabs and fold and attach to the neighboring side.

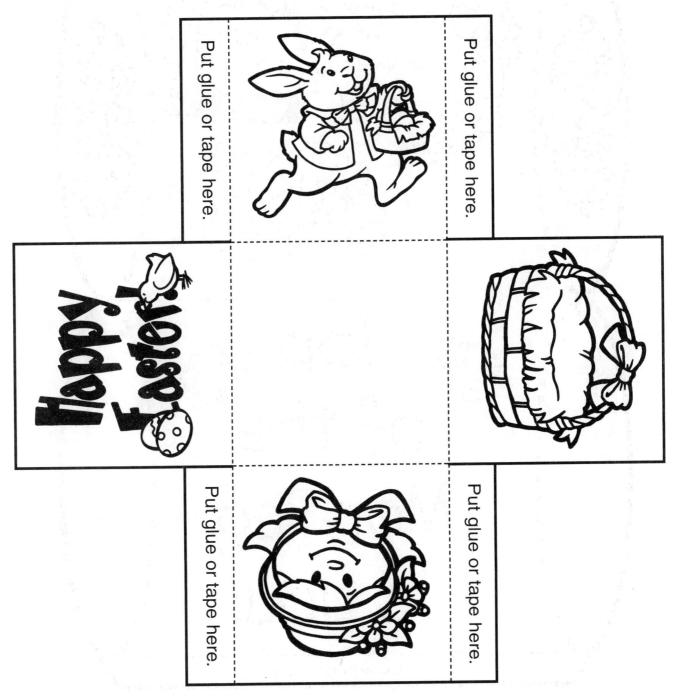

Page 19

True Statements

He was kidnapped and forced to work as a shepherd.

He died on March 17th.

He was a missionary.

False Statements

He was Irish.

He was born on March 17th.

He ate marshmallow charms.

Sample true statement: He was born in Britain.

Page 20

Rabbits

need to be taken care of in the nest

born with closed eyes

born bald

Hares

born with open eyes

can hop soon after being born

born with fur

Sample statement: Hares and rabbits are relatives.

Page 21

1. green
2. leprechaun
3. March
4. pot (of gold)
5. shamrock
6. green
7. leprechaun
8. pot of gold
9. shamrock
10. March

Page 22

1. basket
2. egg
3. grass
4. rabbit
5. spring
6. basket
7. rabbit
8. grass
9. Spring
10. egg

Page 24

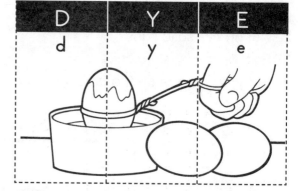

Page 25

Page 26

Page 27

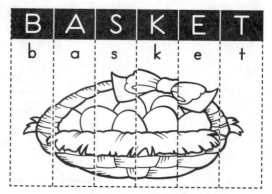

Page 34

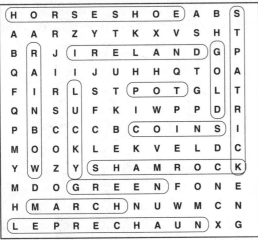

Page 35

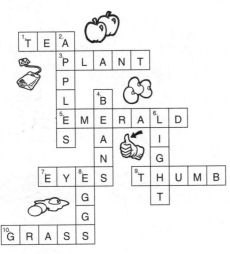

Page 36
1. horseshoe
2. pot
3. shamrock
4. leprechaun
5. rainbow
6. gold

Page 37
1. Air Cell
2. Shell
3. Yolk
4. Chalaza
5. Embryo
6. Albumen

Page 38

Page 39
1. body   4. ear
2. tail   5. nose
3. leg   6. whiskers

Page 50
1. leg   5. see
2. toes   6. cry
3. punt   7. bowl
4. money   8. sick

Page 51
1. mammals   3. Antarctica
2. plants   4. digging

Page 52
1. changes color   3. kangaroo
2. both have long ears   4. hop

Page 53

		Castle	Forest	Rainbow	Mushroom
Liza		X	O	X	X
Paula		X	X	X	O
Rick		X	X	O	X
Will		O	X	X	X

1. Liza found a leprechaun in the <u>forest</u>.
2. Rick found a leprechaun by a <u>rainbow</u>.
3. Paula found a leprechaun by a <u>mushroom</u>.
4. Will found a leprechaun by a <u>castle</u>.

Answer Key *(cont.)*

Page 54

5

Sample Clue: The egg is tied with a bow.

Page 55

  1. Horseshoes: 6

     Moons: 11

     Rainbows: 6

  2. 3

  3. 1

  4. 3

  5. Moon

  6. 5

  7. 3

Page 56

  1. Circle penny.

  2. Circle 2.

  3. Circle rabbit's foot.

  4. Answers will vary.

Page 57

Answers will vary depending on students using marshmallow charms or page 58.

Page 62

  1. 12 cm

  2. 6 cm

  3. 10 cm

  4. 4 cm

  5. 2 cm

Page 65

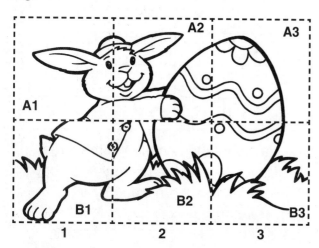

Page 66

Page 67

Page 68

  1. first egg with zig-zag trim

  2. C3

  3. second egg with floral decoration

Weather, Kites, and April Fool's Day

Table of Contents

Introduction

This section (Weather, Kites, and April Fool's Day) contains activities that supplement events that happen in April.

Reading and Language Activities

- **April (page 90):** Simply photocopy the pages the students are to do and use page 90 as a cover for the short unit. Or photocopy the appropriate level of writing paper (pages 6–8) for each student and staple the cover to those pages to make a writing packet.

- **Check-Off List (page 10):** Use the blank check-off list to keep track of each student's language and reading activity as it is completed.

- **April Writing Prompts (pages 91 and 92):** Writing prompts are provided for each one of the four domains. The writing prompts are a fun way for students to explore what they know about weather, kites, and April Fool's Day.

- **About Kites (page 93) and Depending Upon the Weather (page 94):** Students cut out the statements, sort and glue them into the appropriate category. Then students write another true statement about one of the items.

- **Kites (page 95):** Students place kite-related vocabulary words in alphabetical order.

- **Science and Kites (page 96), Clouds (page 97), and Inventions of Benjamin Franklin (page 98):** Students learn different science-related facts from these mini-books. The pages can be cut apart and then stapled together to make a mini-booklet.

- **Letter Matches (pages 99–102):** These cut-and-paste activities reinforce identifying and matching uppercase and lowercase letters. Students cut out the "puzzle pieces" at the bottom of the page and glue them in place under the matching uppercase letter. If done correctly, the letters will spell a word and a picture will be revealed.

- **Making Questions and Statements (page 103):** This activity contains rebus-like pictures and high-frequency words. Students cut apart the words and pictures and arrange and rearrange the words and pictures to make different questions and statements. When doing this activity with the whole class, make an overhead transparency of the pages or use a photocopy machine to enlarge the words and pictures so that they can be easily seen by all of the students.

- **How Many Words Can You Make? (pages 104 and 105):** Students cut apart the letter cards and arrange and rearrange the letters to make different words. When doing this activity with the whole class, make an overhead transparency of the page. Call on individual students to use the overhead to show the class a word they have made. This is also a great activity to send home as homework. Sample words that can be made are as follows:

  The Franklin Page

  Two letters: an, in
  Three letters: ink, fir, kin, fin, ark, Nan
  Four letters: kiln, link, rink, lank, rank, lark
  Five or more letters: Frank

  The Weather Page

  Two letters: at, he, we
  Three letters: are, the, awe, ewe, her, eat
  Four letters: tear, hear, here, wear, wart
  Five or more letters: wheat, there, heart, where

- **Making a Kite (pages 106 and 107):** This rebus story activity uses pictures and high-frequency words to tell a story. Students feel successful when they are able to read the story with little or no help from the teacher!

  The story reads as follows: *One day Bee and Lee made a kite. First, Bee and Lee took two sticks and tied the two sticks together to make a cross. Bee and Lee took string and tied the string to each end of the cross. Bee and Lee put paper on the frame and glued the paper on the string. Bee and Lee tied string to the kite and added a tail.*

- **Weather Word Search (page 108), Rainy Weather (page 109), and Clothes for the Weather (page 110):** Students find vocabulary words about weather in a word search or a crossword puzzle.

- **It's All in the Weather (page 111):** This activity introduces students to weather-related similes and metaphors.

Introduction

Reading and Language Activities *(cont.)*

- **Weather Bingo (pages 112–114):** The bingo game includes eight different bingo cards and matching calling cards. The bingo game reinforces weather-related vocabulary and language development skills in a fun-filled, non-threatening manner

- **About the Weather (page 115) and Parts of a Kite (page 116):** In these activities, students place labels underneath a picture or write the words on a diagram.

- **Compound Words (pages 117–124):** These games introduce and reinforce the concept that a compound word is made from combining two smaller words. Through several different games, students practice this important skill in a concrete manner.

- **April Fool's Day (page 125) and Rainbows (page 126):** These two pages provide students with basic information on these two topics, as well as a few questions for students to answer about what they have just read.

Math Activities

- **Kite Flying (page 127) and Mystery Kite (page 128):** These are logic activities. As each clue is read, students cross off the pictures that meet (or do not meet) the clue.

- **Amazing Kites (page 129):** Students read and answer questions about a chart.

- **This Week's Weather (page 130):** Students construct a graph based on the weather for each school day. At the end of the week, students answer questions about the graph they created.

- **Kite Sales (page 131):** Students read and answer questions about a chart.

- **Today's Temperature (page 132):** Students read a thermometer and then circle the matching temperature.

- **What's the Temperature? (page 133):** Students color a thermometer to show the correct temperature.

- **What Will You Do? (page 134) and What Will You Wear? (page 135):** Students decide on the most appropriate activity or item of clothing based on the temperature.

- **Kite Worth? (pages 136–140):** Students total the value of the different shapes found on each kite. There is a blank kite on page 140 so students can create a kite of a specific value.

- **Follow That Rainbow (page 141), Singing in the Rain (page 142), and Windy Weather (page 143):** Students will glue all the pieces of the puzzle in the correct place on the graph to form a picture.

- **Measure the Umbrellas (page 144):** Students use a centimeter ruler to measure the width of different umbrellas.

- **April Calendar (page 145):** Students put together all the different parts of a calendar and then answer some questions about it.

- **Weather Watching (page 146):** Students identify and locate different weather pictures on the map.

- **Weather Patterns (pages 147 and 148):** Students make patterns using theme-related pictures. Photocopy the pattern sleeve onto construction paper, fold and glue in the back to create the sleeve. For each student, provide three to four 12" lengths of sentence strips. Photocopy a class set of theme-related pictures. Have the students cut out the pictures and use the pictures to make different patterns on the sentence strips.

- **Sun Sort (pages 149 and 150):** This activity can be done with the whole class. Make an overhead transparency of both pages. Place the large cloud on the overhead projector. Place several of the pictures inside the large shape and the remaining pictures outside the shape. Ask the students, "What is the rule to be in this family?" Call on students to answer.

- **Sunny Times Ahead (pages 151–155):** This is a game to reinforce telling time to the half hour. There are several games that the students can play to practice this important concept. The games are ideal for small groups or 2–4 players.

- **Paper Bag Kites (page 156):** Directions are provided so students can make a kite out of a small (or large) paper bag. The kites will really fly if there is just a little wind!

April

April Writing Prompts

Domain	Writing Prompt	Word Bank
Practical/Informative	Write the weather report.	chance of, cloudy, high, low, prediction, seasonal, temperature, today's, tomorrow
Practical/Informative	Make a list of April Fool's Day jokes.	With the students, brainstorm a list of April Fool's Day jokes.
Practical/Informative	How to Make a Kite	cut, fabric, fold, glue, knots, measure, sticks, stretch, string, ribbon, tail, tie
Practical/Informative	Name as many different kites as possible.	With the students, brainstorm a list of the different types of kites they have seen or have read about.
Analytical/Expository	What is the best kind of weather? Why?	beach, clothes, cool, hot, skis, snow, sports, sunny, warm, water, windy
Analytical/Expository	Was it a Good Idea for Benjamin Franklin to Fly a Kite in the Rain?	With the students, brainstorm a list of positives and negatives for flying a kite in the rain.
Analytical/Expository	Should children be allowed to play in the rain?	boots, catch a cold, fun, muddy, puddles, raincoat, splash, umbrella, wet
Analytical/Expository	Should people play jokes on others?	With the students, brainstorm a list of reasons for playing and not playing jokes on others.

April Writing Prompts

Domain	Writing Prompt	Word Bank
Imaginative/Narrative	Describe life as a raindrop.	cloud, fall, grass, plants, plop, puddles, sky, sparkle, splash, tiny, water, wet
Imaginative/Narrative	How to Make a Rainbow	air, arch, bowl, clouds, colors, mix, rain, sky, spoon, stir, stripes, sun, throw
Imaginative/Narrative	What does the earth look like from the point of view of a kite?	colorful, curved, different, patches, people, planet, round, small, tiny, whole
Imaginative/Narrative	You Have Become a Kite. What do you do all day?	entertain, float, fly, laugh, see, string, tail, tickles, travel
Sensory/Descriptive	Describe a cloud.	blows, cotton, floats, light, popcorn, puffy, sky, soft, wet, white, wind
Sensory/Descriptive	Describe a rainbow.	across, arch, clouds, colors, pretty, rain, shines, sparkles, sky, stretches, sun
Sensory/Descriptive	Describe a perfect kite.	colors, dives, fabric, flies, plastic, ribbons, shapes, sticks, tail, tricks
Sensory/Descriptive	How Do You Catch a Sunbeam?	capture, chase, invisible, jar, light, net, outside, sunglasses, sunny, warm

About Kites

Directions: Cut out the boxes at the bottom of the page. Then glue them under the correct title.

Facts	Opinions

Directions: Write another factual statement about kites.

_____

- -

_____

_____

- -

_____

Kites need wind to fly.	Kites have a tail.
Kites are fun to fly.	Kites are pretty.
A kite's frame can be covered with paper, fabric, or plastic.	Only kids can fly kites.

Depending Upon the Weather

Directions: Cut out the boxes at the bottom of the page. Then glue them under the correct title.

Cold Days	Hot Days

Directions: Write a true statement about weather.

_____

- -

_____

_____

- -

_____

go swimming	wear shorts
build a snowman	go skiing
play baseball	wear a jacket

Kites

Directions: Cut out the words at the bottom of the page. Put the words in alphabetical order and then answer each question.

1.

2.

3.

4.

5.

6. Which word is <u>first</u>?

_____

7. Which word comes <u>after</u> *box kite*?

_____

8. Which word comes <u>before</u> *tail*?

_____

9. Which word is <u>last</u>?

_____

10. Which word is in <u>between</u> *frame* and *string*?

_____

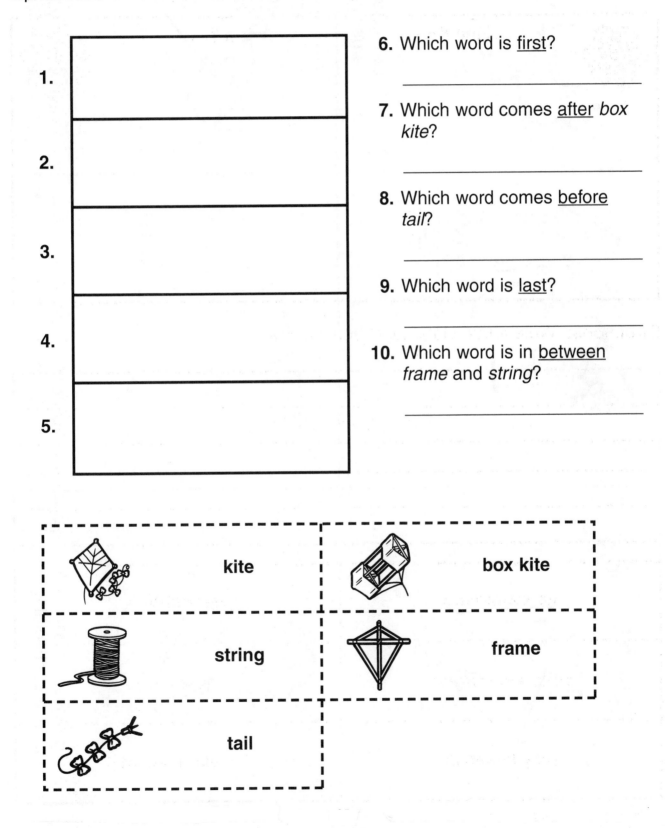

kite

box kite

string

frame

tail

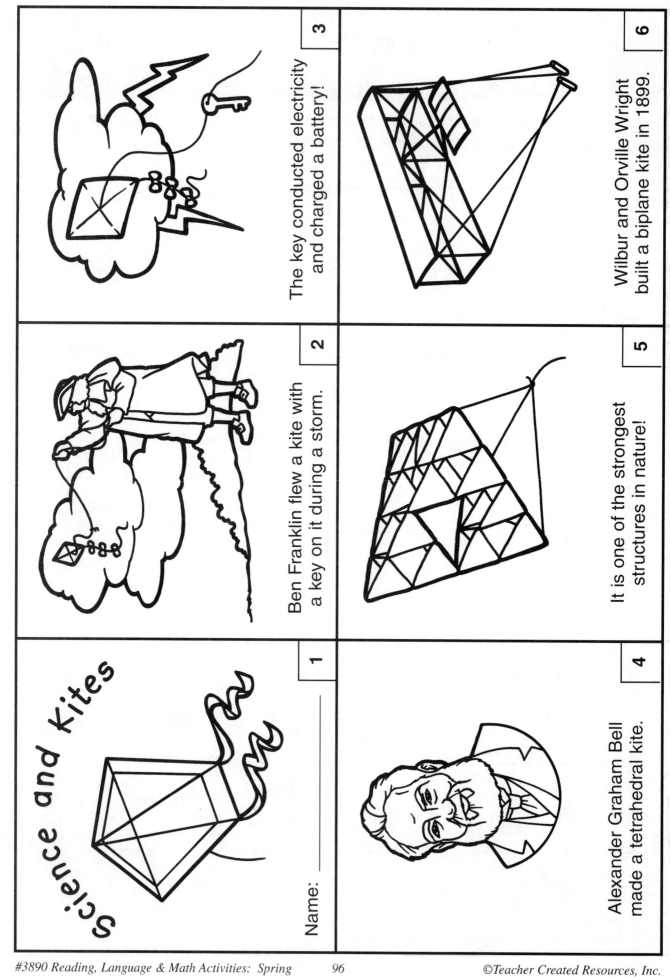

Science and Kites

Name: _____

1

2

Ben Franklin flew a kite with a key on it during a storm.

3

The key conducted electricity and charged a battery!

4

Alexander Graham Bell made a tetrahedral kite.

5

It is one of the strongest structures in nature!

6

Wilbur and Orville Wright built a biplane kite in 1899.

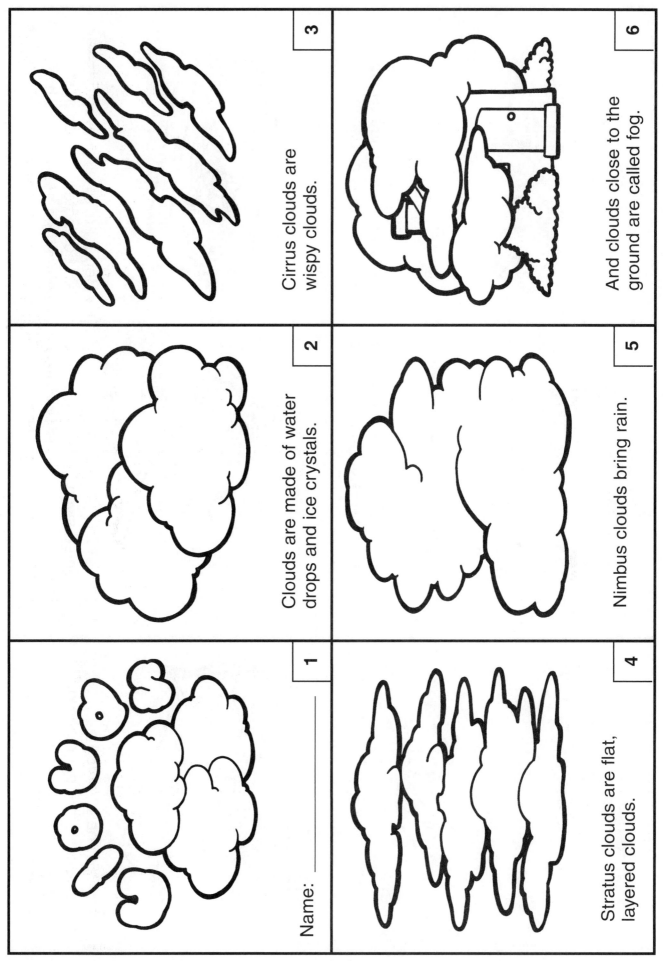

3 Cirrus clouds are wispy clouds.

6 And clouds close to the ground are called fog.

2 Clouds are made of water drops and ice crystals.

5 Nimbus clouds bring rain.

1 Name: _____

4 Stratus clouds are flat, layered clouds.

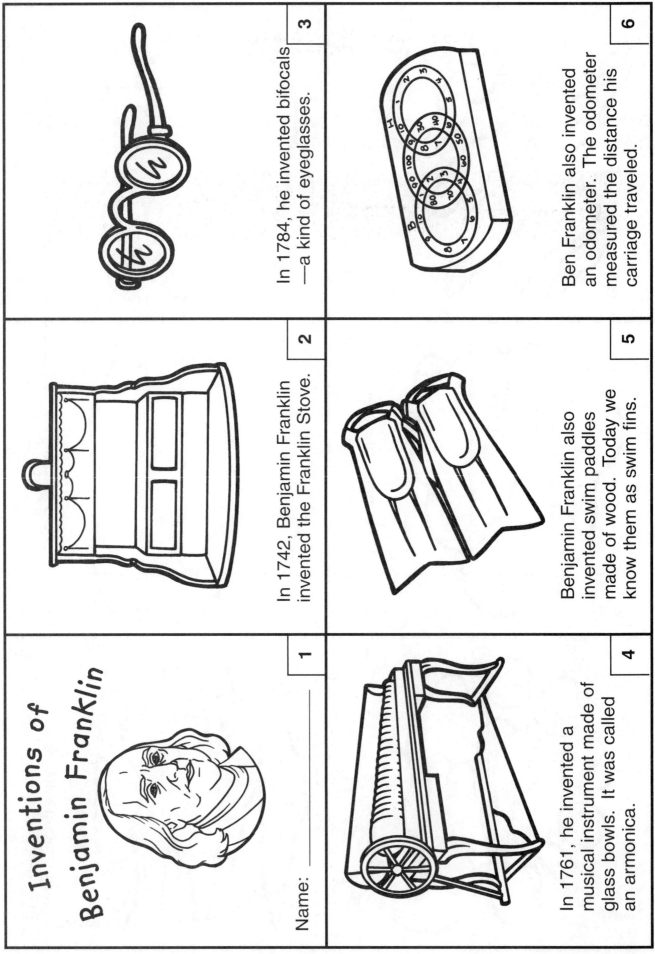

3

In 1784, he invented bifocals —a kind of eyeglasses.

6

Ben Franklin also invented an odometer. The odometer measured the distance his carriage traveled.

2

In 1742, Benjamin Franklin invented the Franklin Stove.

5

Benjamin Franklin also invented swim paddles made of wood. Today we know them as swim fins.

Inventions of Benjamin Franklin

Name: _____

1

4

In 1761, he invented a musical instrument made of glass bowls. It was called an armonica.

Letter Match

Directions: Cut out the boxes at the bottom of the page. Glue the lowercase letter box to the uppercase letter box to find a picture.

W	I	N	D

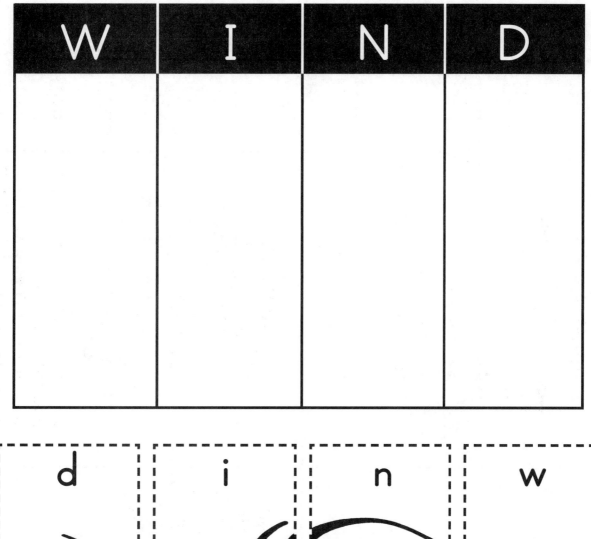

d | i | n | w

Letter Match

Directions: Cut out the boxes at the bottom of the page. Glue the lowercase letter box to the uppercase letter box to find a picture.

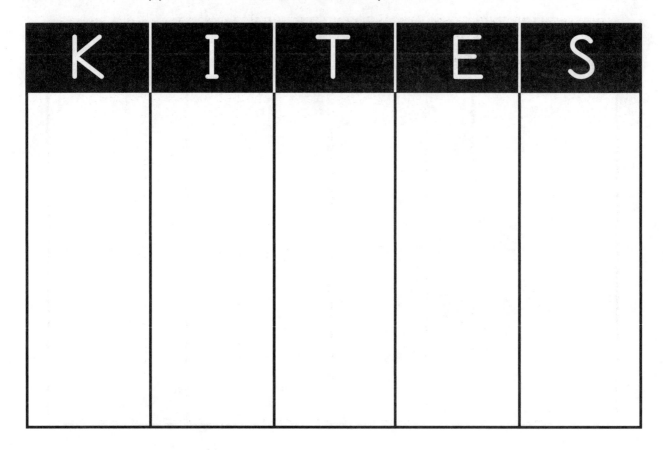

K	I	T	E	S

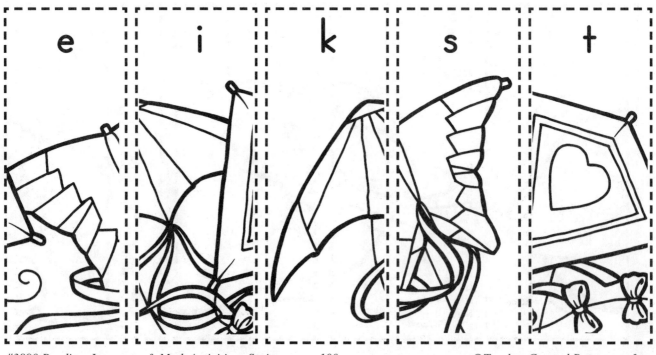

| e | i | k | s | t |

Letter Match

Directions: Cut out the boxes at the bottom of the page. Glue the lowercase letter box to the uppercase letter box to find a picture.

C	L	O	U	D	Y

c	d	l	o	u	y

Letter Match

Directions: Cut out the boxes at the bottom of the page. Glue the lowercase letter box to the uppercase letter box to find a picture.

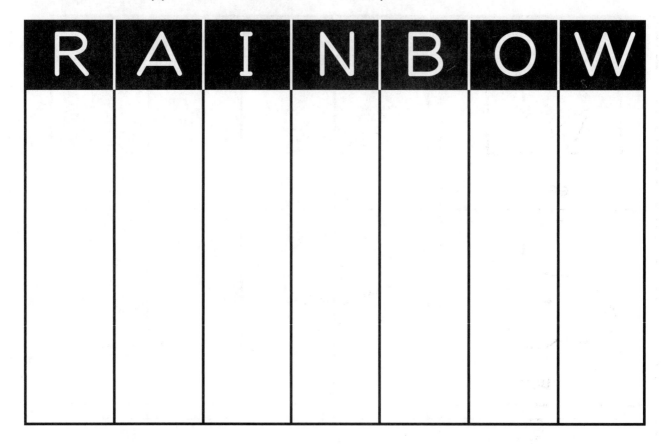

R	A	I	N	B	O	W

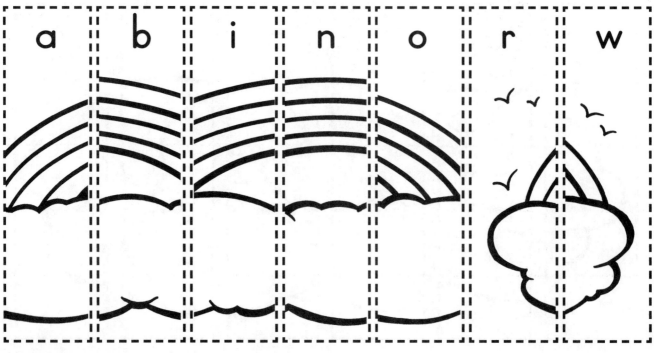

a	b	i	n	o	r	w

Making Questions and Statements

Directions: Cut apart the picture and word cards. Arrange and rearrange the cards to make different questions and statements.

weather	sun	cold
cloudy	rain	hot
windy	snow	What
		is
		the
it	do	like
will	I	How
out	.	?

How Many Words Can You Make?

Directions: Cut out the letters at the bottom of the page. Rearrange the letters to make different words. Write each word under the correct heading.

Two-Letter Words

Three-Letter Words

Four-Letter Words

Five-or-More-Letter Words

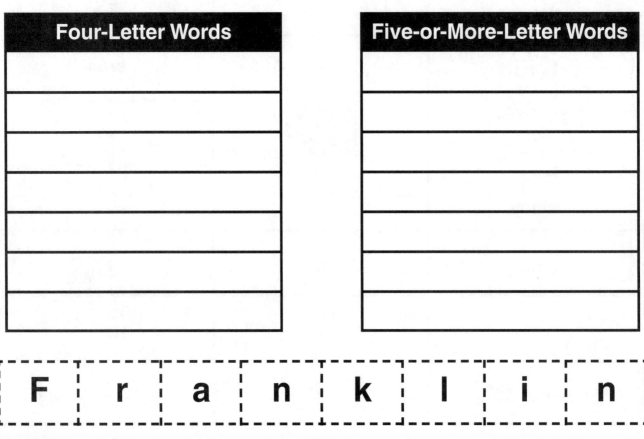

F r a n k l i n

How Many Words Can You Make?

Directions: Cut out the letters at the bottom of the page. Rearrange the letters to make different words. Write each word under the correct heading.

Two-Letter Words

Three-Letter Words

Four-Letter Words

Five-or-More-Letter Words

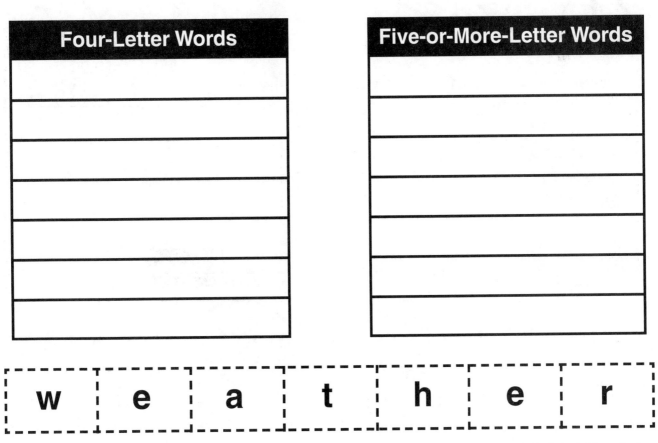

w e a t h e r

Making a Kite

One day Bee and Lee made a

kite. First, Bee and Lee took

 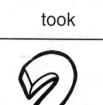

two sticks and tied the two

sticks together to make a

cross. Bee and Lee took

Making a Kite

string   and   tied   the   string   to each

end   of   the   cross.   Bee   and   Lee

put   paper   on   the   frame   and   glued   the

paper   on the   string.   Bee   and   Lee

tied   string   to   the   kite   and   added   a   tail.

Weather Word Search

Directions: Find and color each word in the word search.

COLD	STORM
CLOUDS	SUN
HOT	THUNDER
RAIN	WARM
SNOW	WIND

W	A	T	O	J	N	R	E	U	T
A	W	D	B	Z	R	A	I	N	H
R	Q	D	M	P	S	V	T	K	U
M	Y	I	H	O	T	L	C	S	N
I	W	I	N	D	O	H	B	N	D
S	W	J	S	T	O	R	M	O	E
B	G	S	C	R	X	K	P	W	R
N	U	U	A	X	Z	F	A	L	E
H	Y	N	Q	M	C	C	O	L	D
F	G	V	C	L	O	U	D	S	D

Rainy Weather

Directions: Find and color each word in the word search.

CLOUDBURST   POURING
DOWNPOUR   RAIN
DRIZZLE   SHOWER
FLOOD   SLEET
GENTLE   SPRINKLE
HAIL   STORM

C	L	O	U	D	B	U	R	S	T
A	G	I	S	O	A	H	R	D	S
Q	E	Z	H	W	Z	H	L	R	T
S	N	C	O	N	U	A	G	I	O
L	T	J	W	P	K	I	T	Z	R
E	L	B	E	O	F	L	W	Z	M
E	E	O	R	U	D	B	E	L	R
T	P	O	U	R	I	N	G	E	A
N	F	L	O	O	D	V	D	M	I
C	S	P	R	I	N	K	L	E	N

Clothes for the Weather

Directions: Write the name for each clothing item in the crossword puzzle.

DOWN

1.
2.
3.
5.
6.
8.

BOOTS	SANDALS
HAT	SCARF
JACKET	SUNGLASSES
MITTENS	SWEATER
RAINCOAT	UMBRELLA

ACROSS →

4.
7.
9.
10.

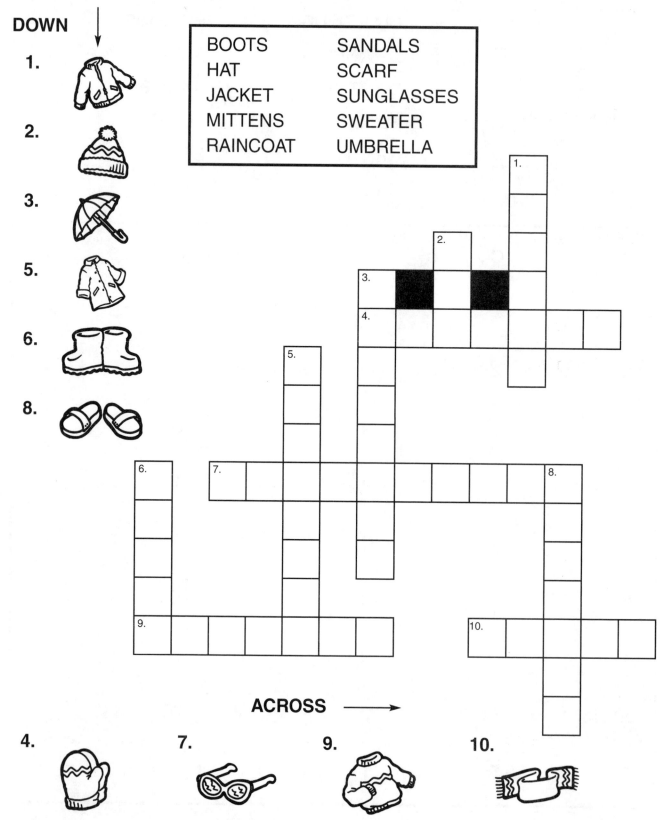

It's All in the Weather

Directions: Draw a line to match each saying with its missing weather word.

snow

1. He is as loud as _____.

rain

2. She is as bright as the noonday _____.

lightning

3. The dog is as white as _____.

thunder

4. It will _____ like cats and dogs.

cold

5. The cat is faster than _____.

sun

6. The man is as _____ as ice.

Weather Bingo

Directions: Photocopy the calling cards below onto cardstock, color, laminate, and cut apart. Provide each student with a game board (pages 113 and 114) and some counters (beans, pennies, multilinks, etc.). Mix up the calling cards. As each card is read aloud, have students cover the matching picture on their boards with a counter. The first student to get three in a row (vertically, horizontally, or diagonally) wins the game.

cloudy	sunny	puddles
windy	rain	rainbow
windy	rain	rainbow
hot	temperature	snow

Weather Bingo

Card 1

Weather Bingo

cloudy	snow	rainbow
hot	Free Space	windy
rain	sunny	storm

Card 2

Weather Bingo

temperature	puddles	storm
snow	Free Space	cloudy
windy	lightning	rainbow

Card 3

Weather Bingo

storm	sunny	snow
rain	Free Space	puddles
rainbow	cloudy	cold

Card 4

Weather Bingo

windy	hot	sunny
cold	Free Space	rain
puddles	temperature	lightning

Weather Bingo

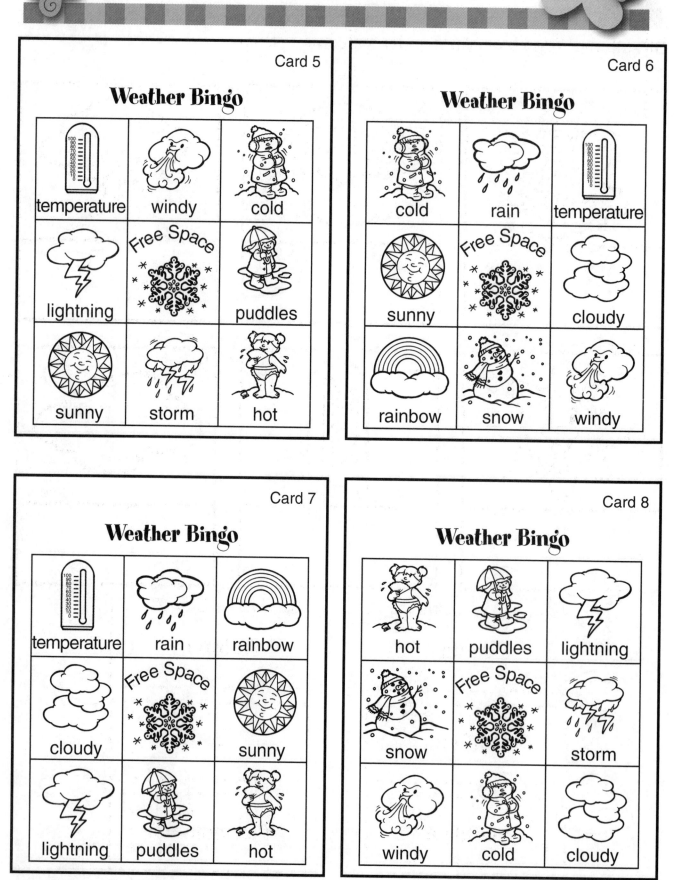

Card 5

Weather Bingo

temperature	windy	cold
lightning	Free Space	puddles
sunny	storm	hot

Card 6

Weather Bingo

cold	rain	temperature
sunny	Free Space	cloudy
rainbow	snow	windy

Card 7

Weather Bingo

temperature	rain	rainbow
cloudy	Free Space	sunny
lightning	puddles	hot

Card 8

Weather Bingo

hot	puddles	lightning
snow	Free Space	storm
windy	cold	cloudy

About the Weather

Directions: Glue each word under the correct picture.

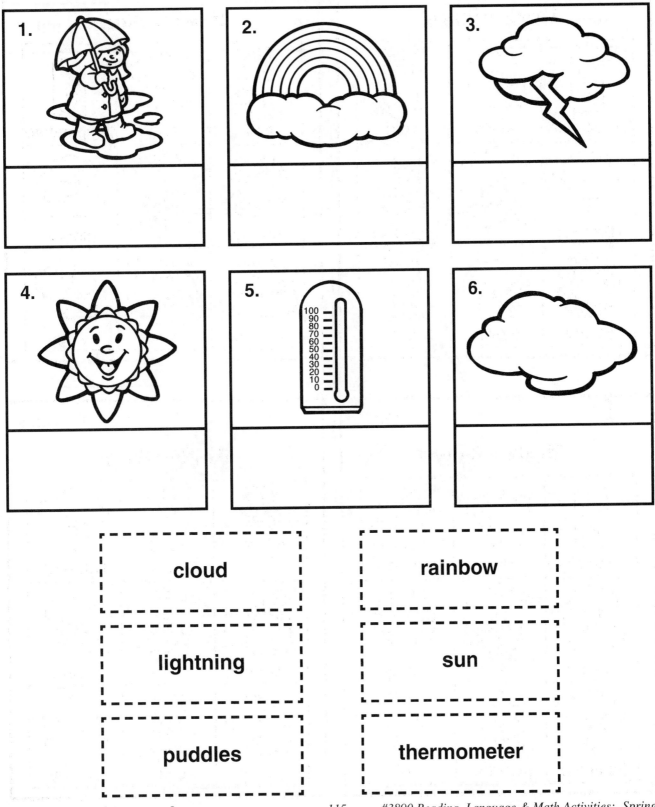

cloud

rainbow

lightning

sun

puddles

thermometer

Parts of a Kite

Directions: Write each word in the correct place on the diagram.

cover	frame	line	reel	tail

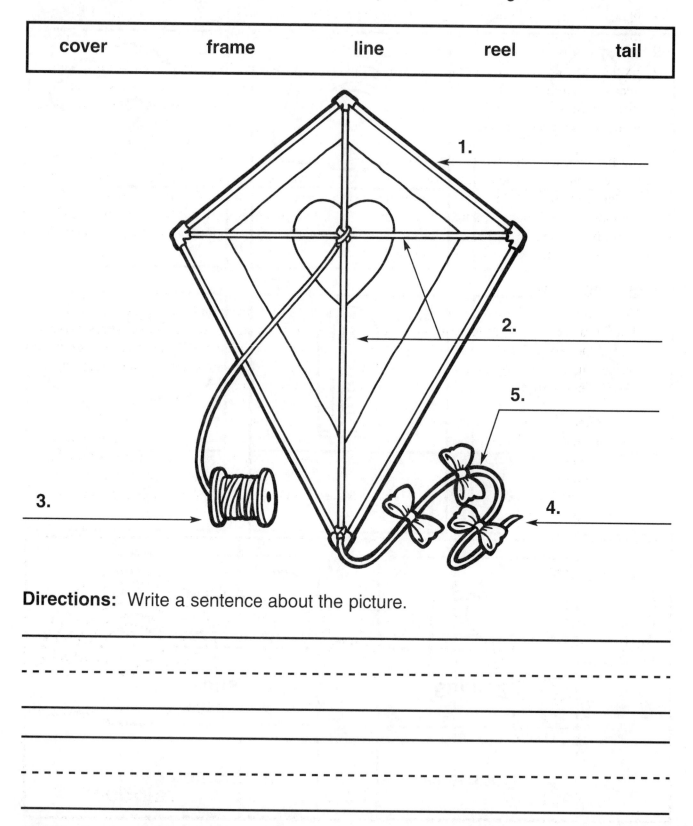

1.

2.

5.

3.

4.

Directions: Write a sentence about the picture.

Compound Words

Directions

- Photocopy the compound word cards (pages 117–120) onto cardstock. (*Management tip:* Photocopy the actual compound words—*weatherman, downpour,* etc.—onto a different color of cardstock.)

- Explain to students that a compound word is made up of two smaller words, such as *turtle* and *neck* combining to make *turtleneck.* Show students each compound word card and ask them to identify the smaller words within the compound word. (Example: *weatherman*—The two smaller words are *weather* and *man.*

- Shuffle the individual word cards together (leaving out the compound words) and place in a stack face down on the table and turn over the top card. Have a student turn over the next card. If the student can combine his or her card with the card already showing on the table to make a compound word, he or she may take both cards. If the student is unable to make a compound word, he or she leaves the card face down on the table. Play continues with the next student. The student with the most pairs of compound words wins the game.

Other Game Ideas

- Concentration: Shuffle the individual word cards together and lay them face down on the table in a 4 x 5 arrangement. Taking turns, each student turns over two cards. If the pair of words make a compound word, the student can keep both cards and take another turn. If the words do not make a compound word, the student turns them back over and play continues with the next student. The student with the most pairs of compound words wins the game.

- Compound 9: Using all of the cards, shuffle them together and lay them face up in a 3 x 3 arrangement. The student then finds any sets of compound words showing in the arrangement— all three cards are needed. Example: *down, pour,* and *downpour.* Once the player has found all the compound word sets, the empty spaces are filled in with the remaining cards and play continues with the next student. If no matches can be made, then all of the cards are removed and fresh cards are laid out.

| rain | bow | rainbow |

Compound Words

weather

man

weatherman

down

pour

downpour

ice

box

icebox

Compound Words

rain

coat

raincoat

snow

flake

snowflake

star

fish

starfish

Compound Words

sun	burn	sunburn
wind	mill	windmill
air	bag	airbag

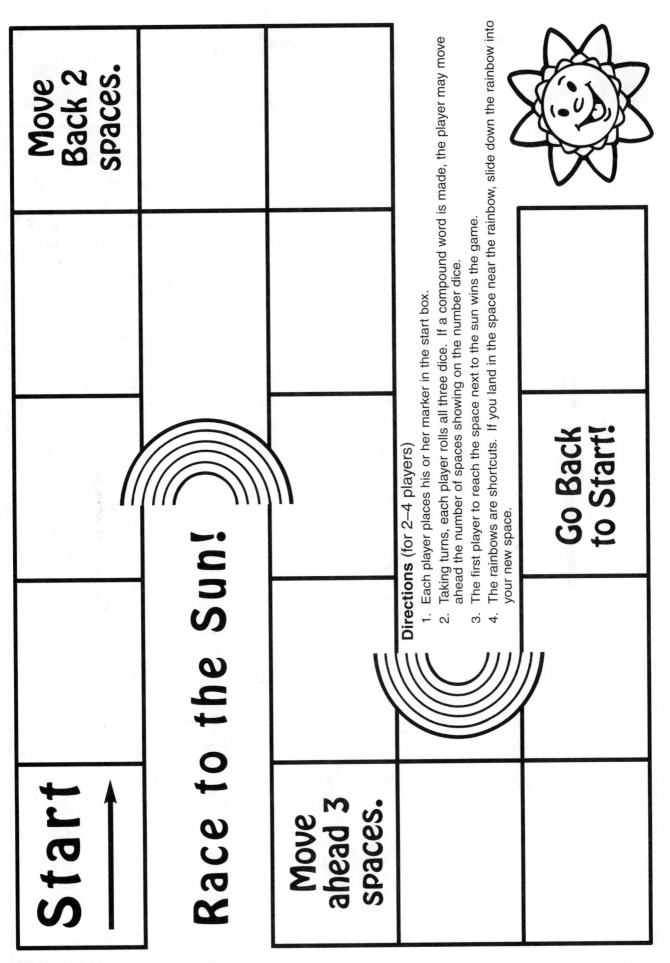

Start →

Race to the Sun!

Move Back 2 spaces.

Move ahead 3 spaces.

Go Back to Start!

Directions (for 2–4 players)

1. Each player places his or her marker in the start box.
2. Taking turns, each player rolls all three dice. If a compound word is made, the player may move ahead the number of spaces showing on the number dice.
3. The first player to reach the space next to the sun wins the game.
4. The rainbows are shortcuts. If you land in the space near the rainbow, slide down the rainbow into your new space.

Compound Word Dice

Assembly Instructions

1. Cut along all solid lines (including around large tabs).

2. Fold along all dashed lines.

3. Glue tab A to inside edge of side D.

4. Fold in top and bottom flaps.

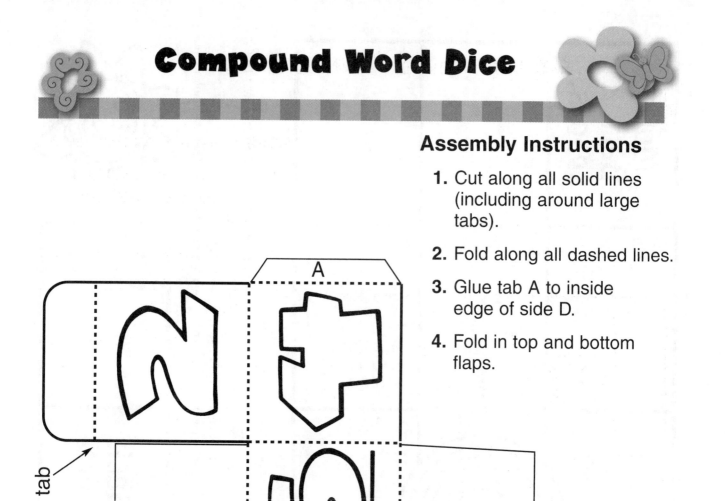

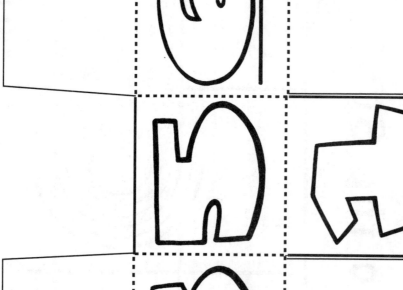

Compound Word Dice

Assembly Instructions

1. Cut along all solid lines (including around large tabs).

2. Fold along all dashed lines.

3. Glue tab A to inside edge of side D.

4. Fold in top and bottom flaps.

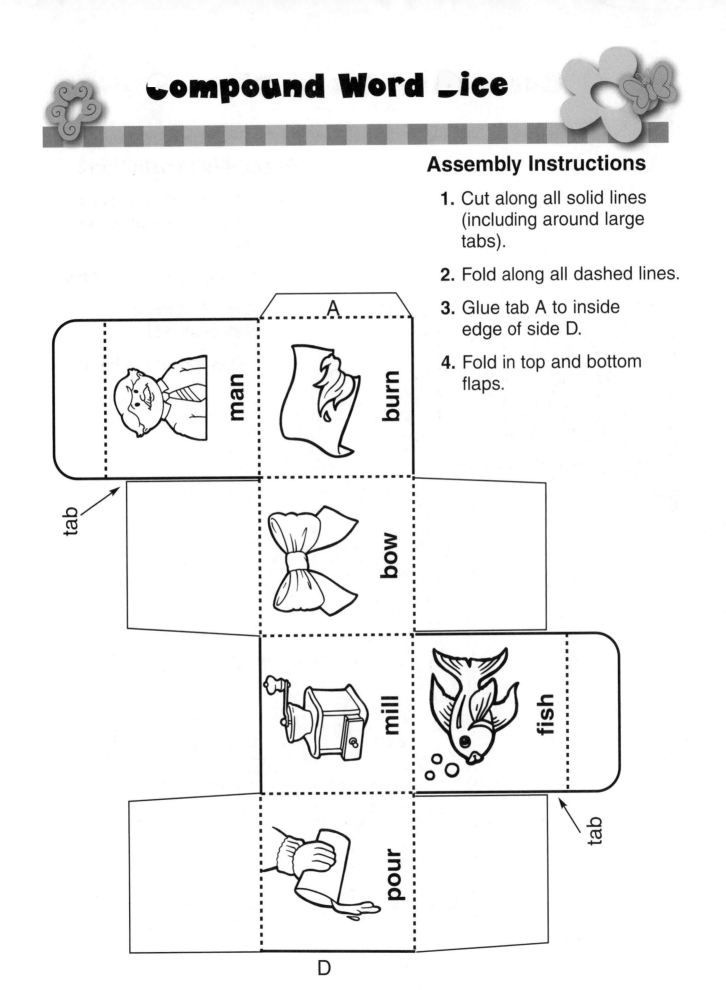

Compound Word Dice

Assembly Instructions

1. Cut along all solid lines (including around large tabs).

2. Fold along all dashed lines.

3. Glue tab A to inside edge of side D.

4. Fold in top and bottom flaps.

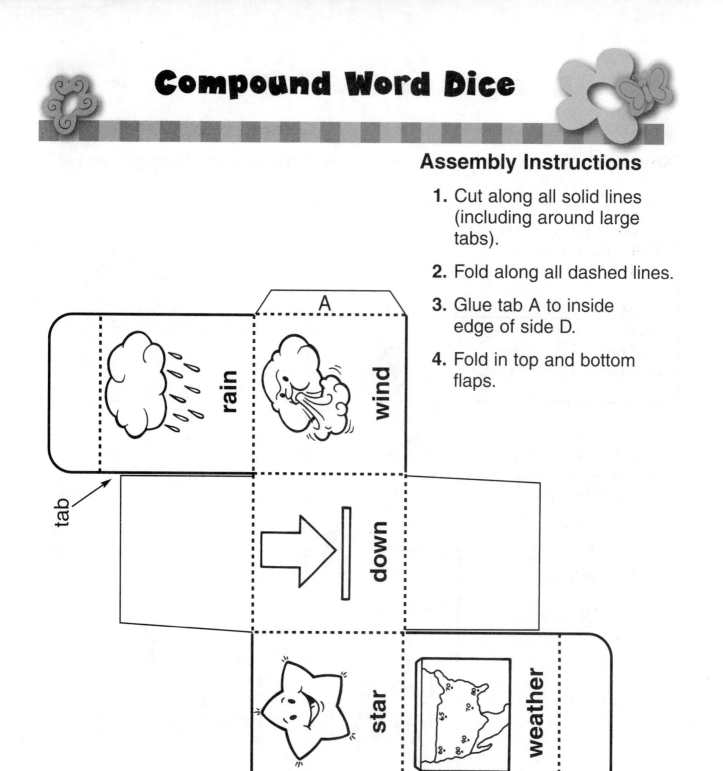

April Fool's Day

Directions: Read the information in the box and answer the questions below.

During the 1500's, the calendar was changed. The official start of the new year was moved from April 1st to January 1st.

Some people still celebrated the new year on April 1st. These people were thought to be "fools" and had jokes played on them. They were given invitations to fake parties and were given gag gifts.

1. Today, when is the new year celebrated?

December 1 ◯   January 1 ◯   April 1 ◯

2. Hundreds of years ago, when was the new year celebrated?

December 1 ◯   January 1 ◯   April 1 ◯

3. When people celebrated the new year on April 1st, what were they called?

happy ◯   friendly ◯   fools ◯

4. What were the "fools" given?

fake invitations ◯   fake food ◯   fake jewelry ◯

Rainbows

Directions: Read the information in the box and answer the questions below.

A rainbow is made when rain falls in one part of the sky and the sun is shining in another part of the sky. That is why we see rainbows when it is raining and the sun is out too! The colors in the rainbow are red, orange, yellow, green, blue, indigo, and violet.

When a rainbow is seen from the ground, it makes a half-circle. But from up in an airplane, the rainbow makes a full circle!

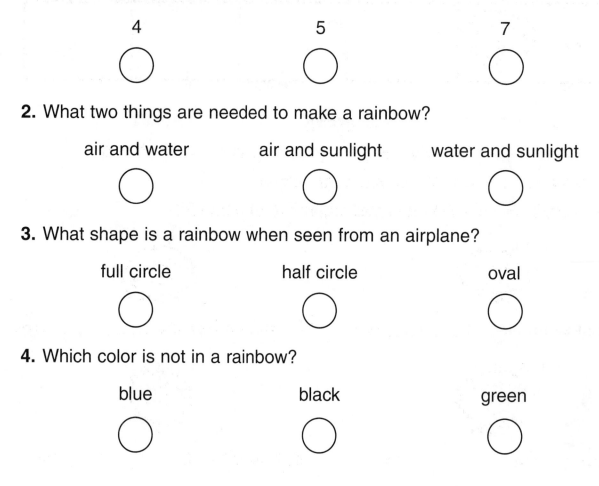

1. How many colors are in a rainbow?

4	5	7
◯	◯	◯

2. What two things are needed to make a rainbow?

air and water	air and sunlight	water and sunlight
◯	◯	◯

3. What shape is a rainbow when seen from an airplane?

full circle	half circle	oval
◯	◯	◯

4. Which color is not in a rainbow?

blue	black	green
◯	◯	◯

Kite Flying

Directions: Read each clue. If the answer is "yes," make an **O** in the box. If the answer is "no," make an **X** in the box. Then complete the statements below.

	square kite	cartoon kite	diamond kite	dragon kite
Andrea				
Joey				
Noreen				
Trevor				

CLUES

- Noreen flies a kite with the name that begins with the letter **d**.
- Joey flies a kite in the shape of an animal.
- Andrea flies a kite that is also the name of a shape.

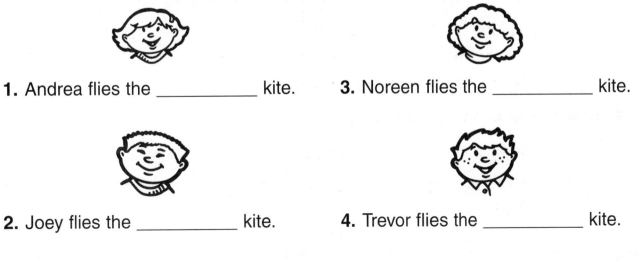

1. Andrea flies the _____ kite.   **3.** Noreen flies the _____ kite.

2. Joey flies the _____ kite.   **4.** Trevor flies the _____ kite.

Mystery Kite

Directions: Read the clues. Cross off the pictures that do not fit the clues.

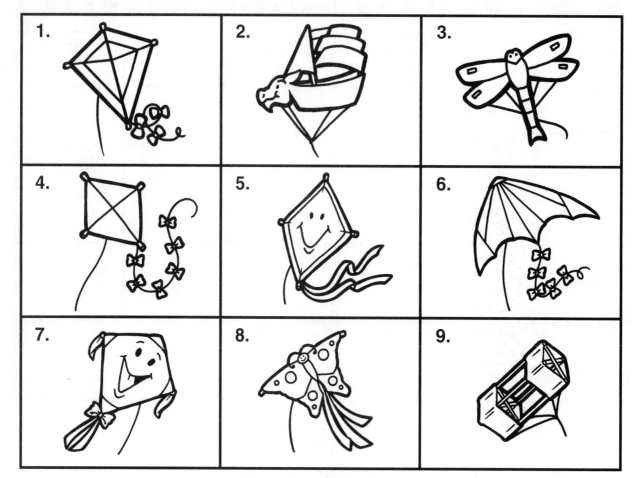

CLUES

- The kite has a tail.
- The kite has more than four bows on its tail.
- The kite does not have a face.
- The kite frame has four triangles.

Which kite did Benjamin Franklin fly? _____

Directions: Write another clue that would fit the mystery kite.

_____

- -

Amazing Kites

Directions: Use the graph to answer the questions.

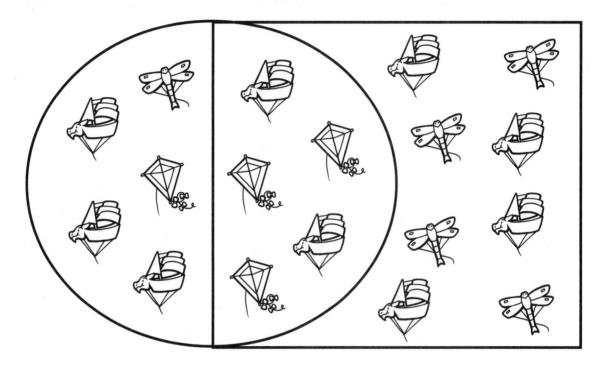

1. How many of each item are shown on the chart?

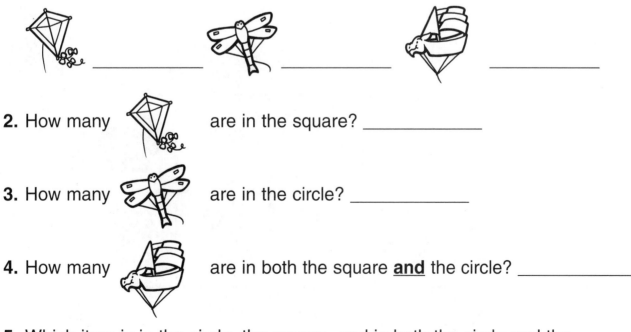

_____   _____   _____

2. How many [kite] are in the square? _____

3. How many [dragonfly] are in the circle? _____

4. How many [kite with sail] are in both the square **and** the circle? _____

5. Which item is in the circle, the square, and in both the circle and the square? _____

This Week's Weather

Directions: Cut the pictures out at the bottom of the page. Glue them to the graph. Then use the pictures to answer the question about the weather for the week.

Sunny						
Rainy						
Snowy						

1. Which kind of weather occurred the most often?

2. Which kind of weather occurred the least often?

3. Was it mostly ☀ or 💧 this week?

4. What is your favorite kind of weather?

Kite Sales

Directions: Use the graph to answer the questions.

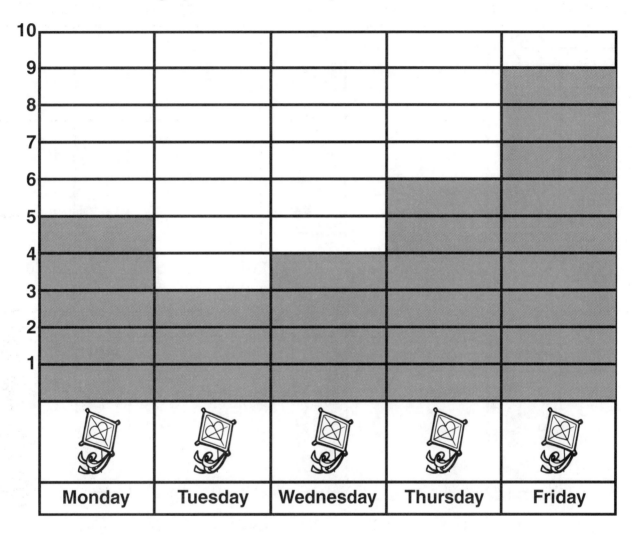

1. On which day were four kites sold? _____

2. On which day were the most kites sold? _____

3. On which day were the fewest kites sold? _____

4. How many kites were sold on Monday? _____

5. How many kites were sold on Thursday? _____

6. How many kites were sold in all? _____

Today's Temperature

Directions: Read the temperature on each thermometer. Circle the correct temperature.

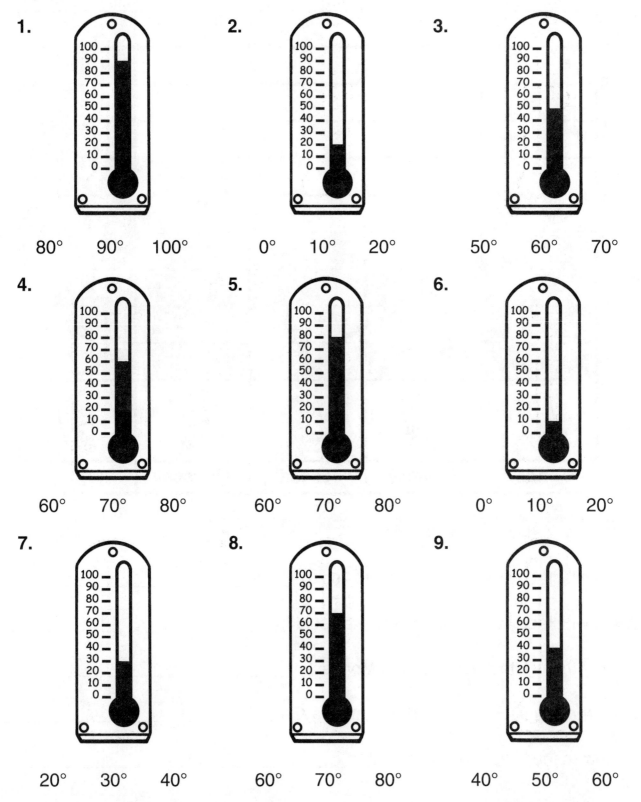

1.

80°   90°   100°

2.

0°   10°   20°

3.

50°   60°   70°

4.

60°   70°   80°

5.

60°   70°   80°

6.

0°   10°   20°

7.

20°   30°   40°

8.

60°   70°   80°

9.

40°   50°   60°

What's the Temperature?

Directions: Color to show each temperature.

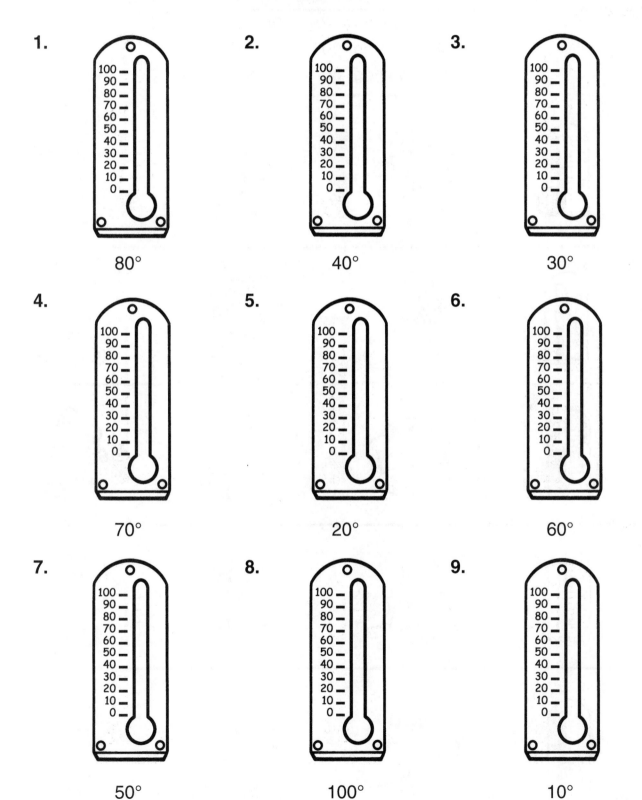

1.   80°

2.   40°

3.   30°

4.   70°

5.   20°

6.   60°

7.   50°

8.   100°

9.   10°

What Will You Do?

Directions: Circle the activity or activities that fit each temperature.

- warm weather 75°–90°
- cool weather 60°–75°
- cold weather 60° or lower

1.

2.

3.

4.

5.

What Will You Wear?

Directions: Circle the clothing item or items that fit each temperature.

- warm weather 75°–90°
- cool weather 60°–75°
- cold weather 60° or lower

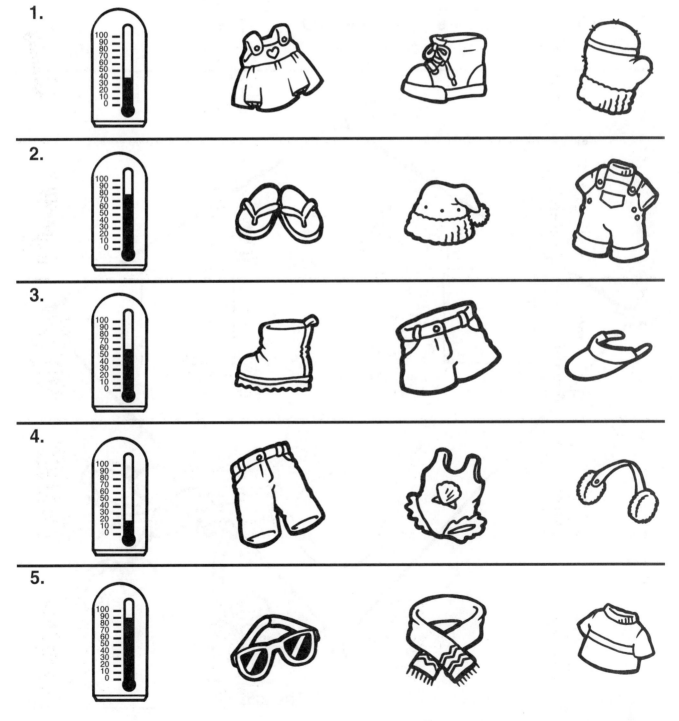

1.

2.

3.

4.

5.

Directions: Use the chart below to find the value of each kite. (*Hint:* Use paper, plastic, or real coins to help in figuring out each kite's value.)

circle	square	diamond	star	heart
1¢	2¢	3¢	5¢	10¢

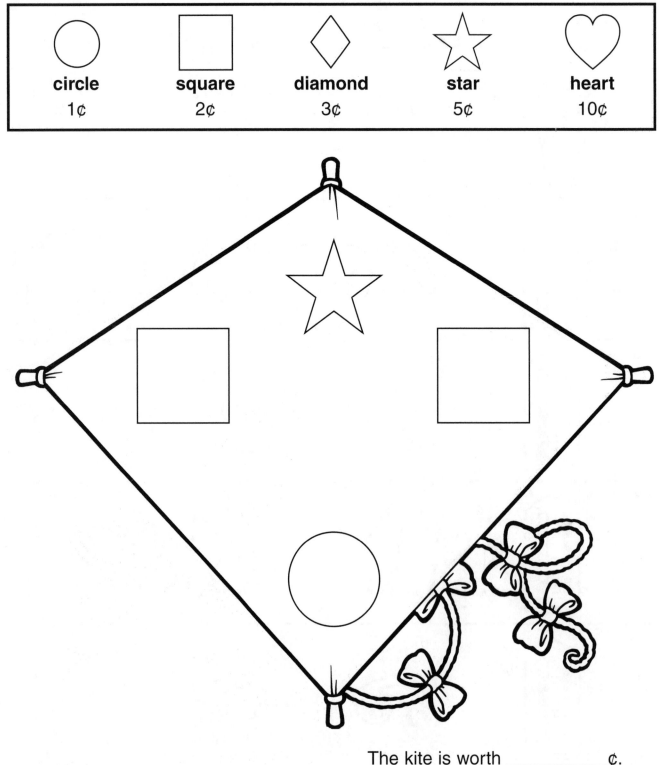

The kite is worth _____ ¢.

Kite Worth? #2

Directions: Use the chart below to find the value of each kite. (*Hint:* Use paper, plastic, or real coins to help in figuring out each kite's value.)

circle	square	diamond	star	heart
1¢	2¢	3¢	5¢	10¢

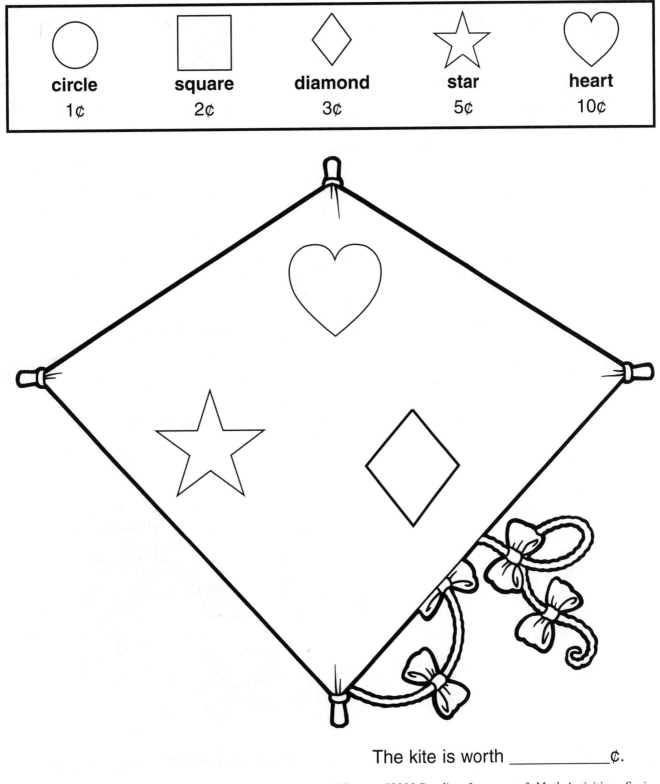

The kite is worth _____ ¢.

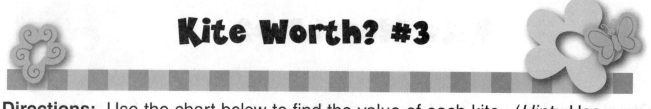

Directions: Use the chart below to find the value of each kite. (*Hint:* Use paper, plastic, or real coins to help in figuring out each kite's value.)

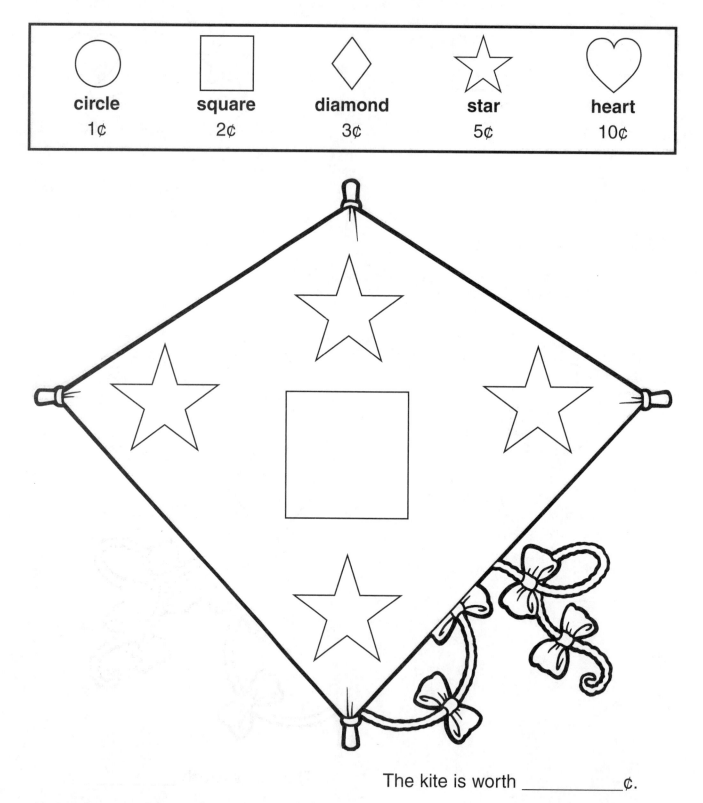

circle	square	diamond	star	heart
1¢	2¢	3¢	5¢	10¢

The kite is worth _____ ¢.

Kite Worth? #4

Directions: Use the chart below to find the value of each kite. (*Hint:* Use paper, plastic, or real coins to help in figuring out each kite's value.)

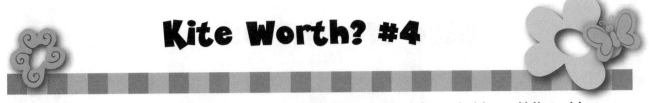

circle	square	diamond	star	heart
1¢	2¢	3¢	5¢	10¢

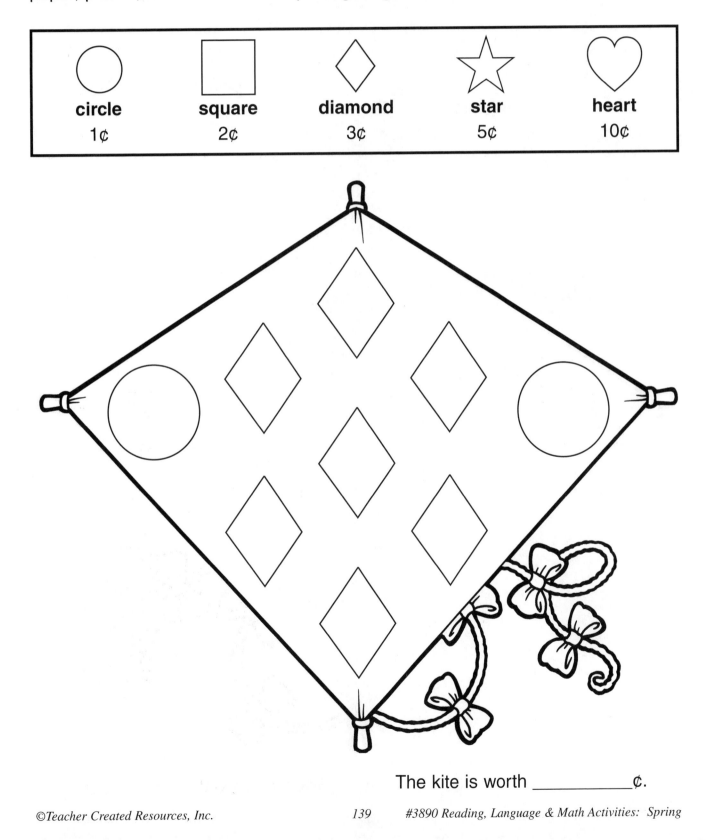

The kite is worth _____¢.

Kite Worth? #5

Directions: Use the chart below to make a value of a kite. Then let a partner try and solve your value.

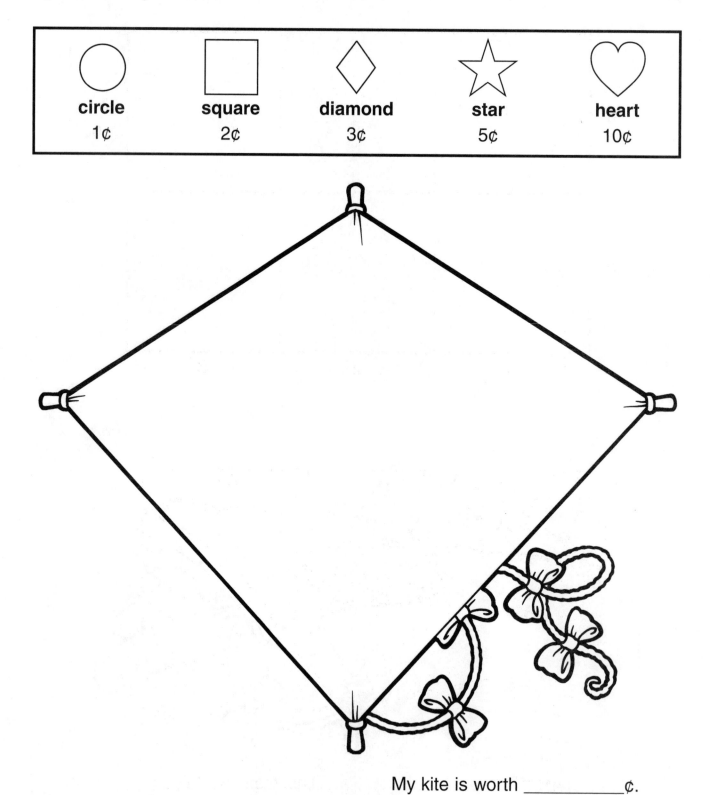

circle	square	diamond	star	heart
1¢	2¢	3¢	5¢	10¢

My kite is worth _____ ¢.

Follow That Rainbow

Directions: Cut out the pieces at the bottom of the page. Glue each puzzle piece in the correct space on the graph.

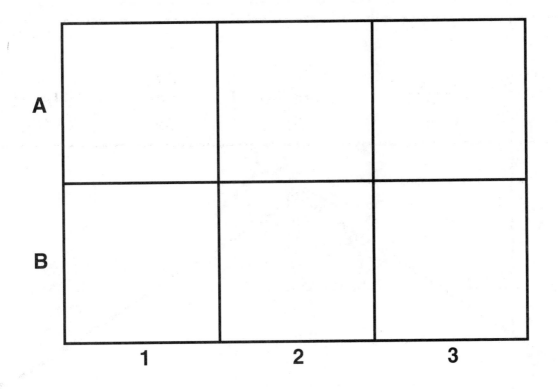

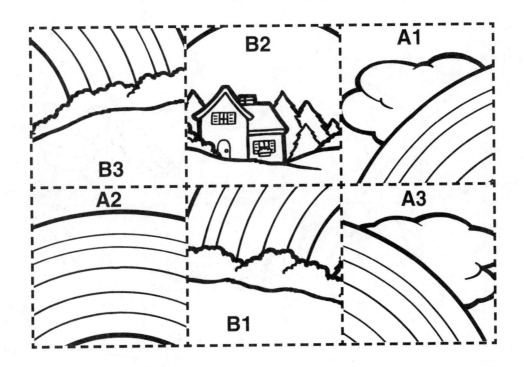

Singing in the Rain

Directions: Cut out the pieces at the bottom of the page. Glue each puzzle piece in the correct space on the graph.

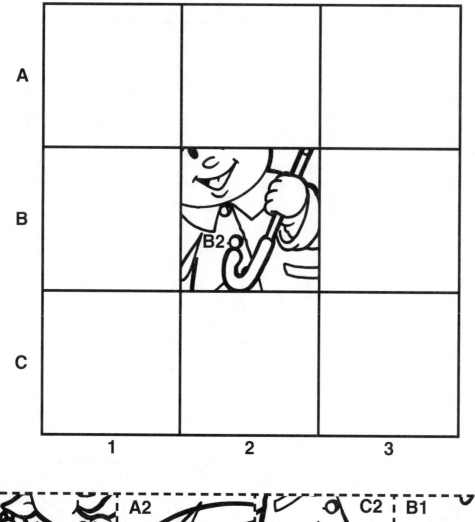

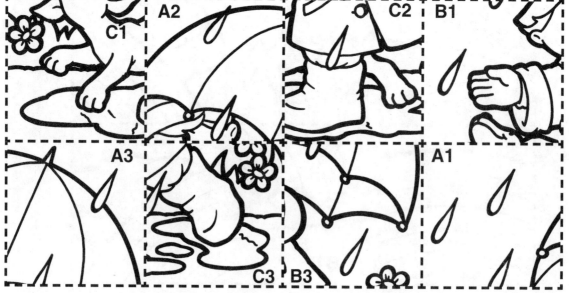

Windy Weather

Directions: Cut out the pieces at the bottom of the page. Glue each puzzle piece in the correct space on the graph.

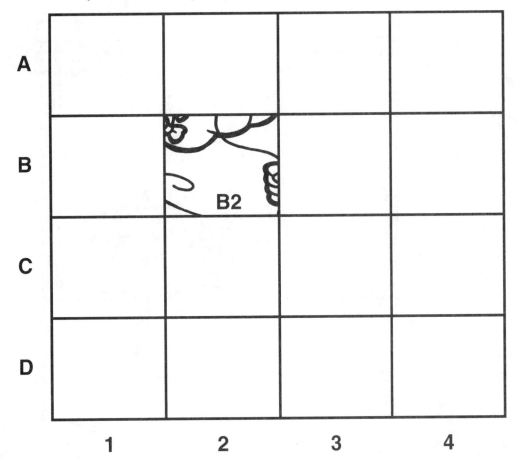

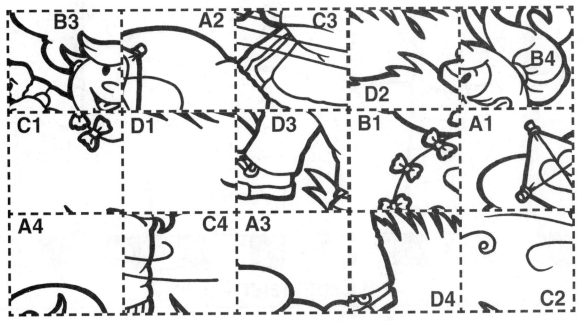

Measure the Umbrellas

Directions: Cut out the ruler at the bottom. Measure the width of each umbrella to the nearest centimeter (cm).

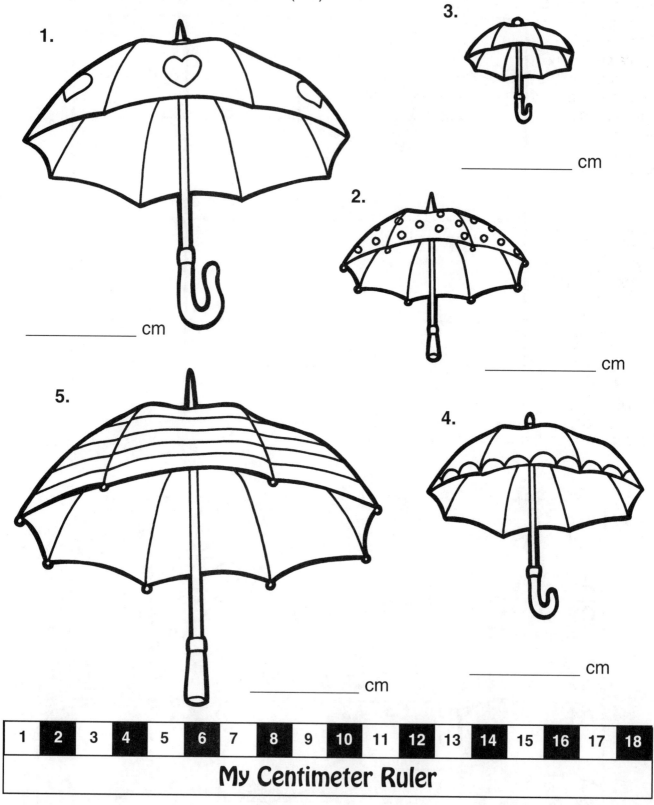

1.

_____ cm

3.

_____ cm

2.

_____ cm

5.

_____ cm

4.

_____ cm

| 1 | 2 | 3 | 4 | 5 | 6 | 7 | 8 | 9 | 10 | 11 | 12 | 13 | 14 | 15 | 16 | 17 | 18 |

My Centimeter Ruler

April Calendar

Directions: Photocopy the blank calendar (page 64) and this page. Make a clean copy of the calendar fill-in section first on this page and add any special school or local events in the empty squares. Students' names can be added to the birthday squares. Then photocopy the completed "fill-in" page. Have students add the month and the days of the week to the calendar. Students also can write the current year next to the name of the month. Have students write the calendar numbers in each square. Have students add the special squares to the appropriate dates on the calendar. Using markers or crayons, have students color the calendar. Have students answer the questions about the calendar.

(*Optional Step:* Fold a 12" x 18" inch piece of colored construction paper in half which would be 12" x 9". Have students open the folded piece of construction paper and glue or staple the completed calendar to the bottom half of the paper. On the top half, have students draw a picture for the current month.)

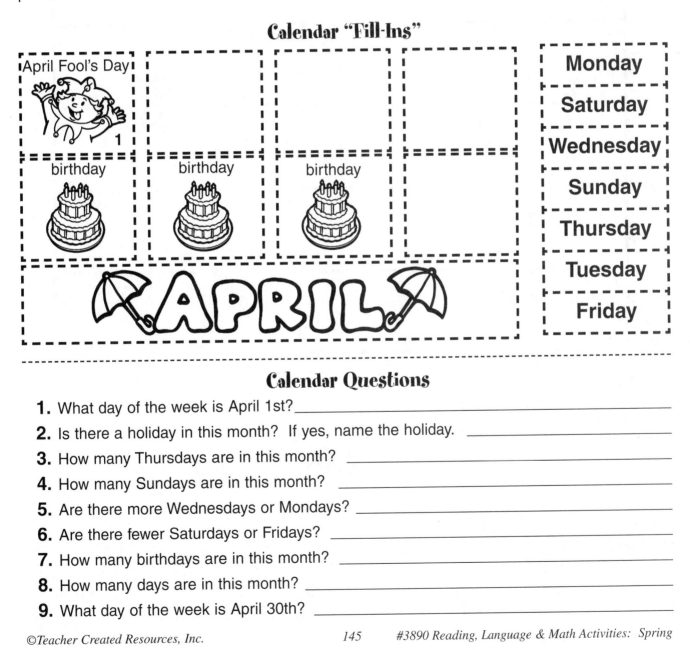

Calendar "Fill-Ins"

Calendar Questions

1. What day of the week is April 1st?_____

2. Is there a holiday in this month? If yes, name the holiday. _____

3. How many Thursdays are in this month? _____

4. How many Sundays are in this month? _____

5. Are there more Wednesdays or Mondays? _____

6. Are there fewer Saturdays or Fridays? _____

7. How many birthdays are in this month? _____

8. How many days are in this month? _____

9. What day of the week is April 30th? _____

Weather Watching

Directions: Use the map to answer the questions.

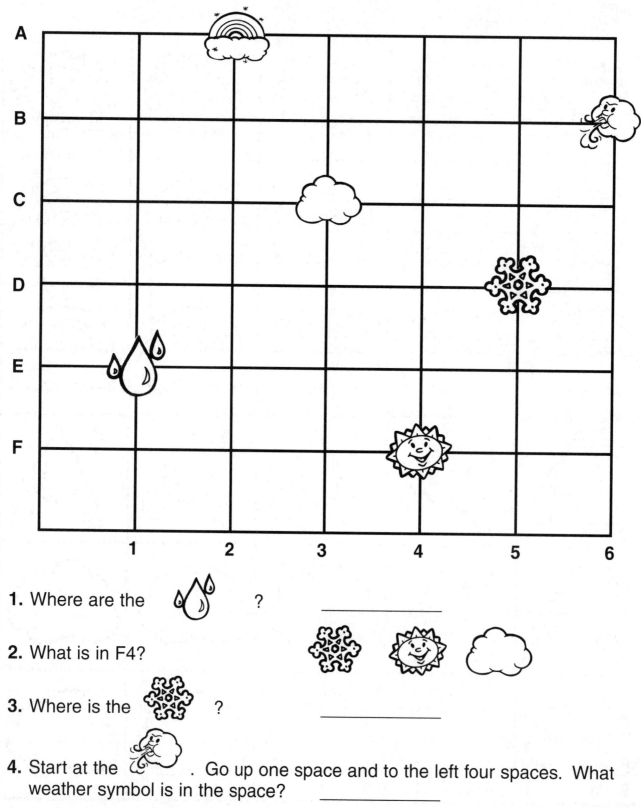

1. Where are the ⬤ ? _____

2. What is in F4? ❄ ☀ ☁

3. Where is the ❄ ? _____

4. Start at the ☁ . Go up one space and to the left four spaces. What weather symbol is in the space? _____

Weather Patterns

Directions: Photocopy a class set of this page onto white construction paper. Have students color and cut out the squares and arrange the squares into different patterns. Glue the squares onto a 12" long sentence strip.

Weather Patterns

Name: _____

Sun Sorting

Directions: Cut out the sun pictures. Use the cloud (page 150) to find the different ways the sun can be sorted.

Sun Sorting

Directions: Put the suns (page 149) that have something in common into the cloud.

To be in this family _____.

Sunny Times Ahead
(Game #1)

Directions: Photocopy two sets of the cards onto colored cardstock. (*Management tip:* Photocopy the hours and numbers on one color of cardstock and the word cards on a different color of cardstock.)

To play:

1. Have each player assemble his or her board (page 155). Provide each player with nine markers.
2. Shuffle the hour cards and place in a stack face down on the table.
3. Shuffle the word cards and place in a separate stack face down on the table.
4. Turn over the top card from each stack.
5. Have players cover the matching time on their playing boards. The first player to get three in a row (either vertically, horizontally, or diagonally) wins the game.

half past _____ (name the hour)	thirty minutes after _____ (name the hour)	_____ o'clock (name the hour)
_____ on the (name the hour) hour	half past _____ (name the hour)	_____ on the (name the hour) hour
1	2	3
4	5	6
7	8	9
10	11	12

Sunny Times Ahead
(Game #2)

Directions

1. Photocopy the clocks (pages 152–154) onto cardstock and cut apart.
2. Have each player assemble his or her board (page 155). Provide each player with nine markers.
3. Shuffle the clock cards and place in a stack face down on the table.
4. Turn over the top card. Have a student identify the time. Have players cover the matching time on their playing boards. The first player to get three in a row (either vertically, horizontally, or diagonally) wins the game.

Extension Activity #1: Make two sets of the clocks and play concentration. Shuffle the cards and lay them face down in a 6 x 8 arrangement. Taking turns, have a player turn over two cards. If the clocks show the same time, the player keeps both cards and takes another turn. If the clocks do not show the same time, the player turns the cards back over and play continues with the next player. The player with the most cards wins the game.

Extension Activity #2: Place the clocks in a pocket chart. Have students arrange the clocks in sequential order starting with 1:00.

Sunny Times Ahead
(Game #2)

Sunny Times Ahead
(Game #2)

Sunny Times Ahead

Directions: Cut out the times at the bottom of the page. Select nine of the times to place on the suns. The first player to get three in a row wins the game.

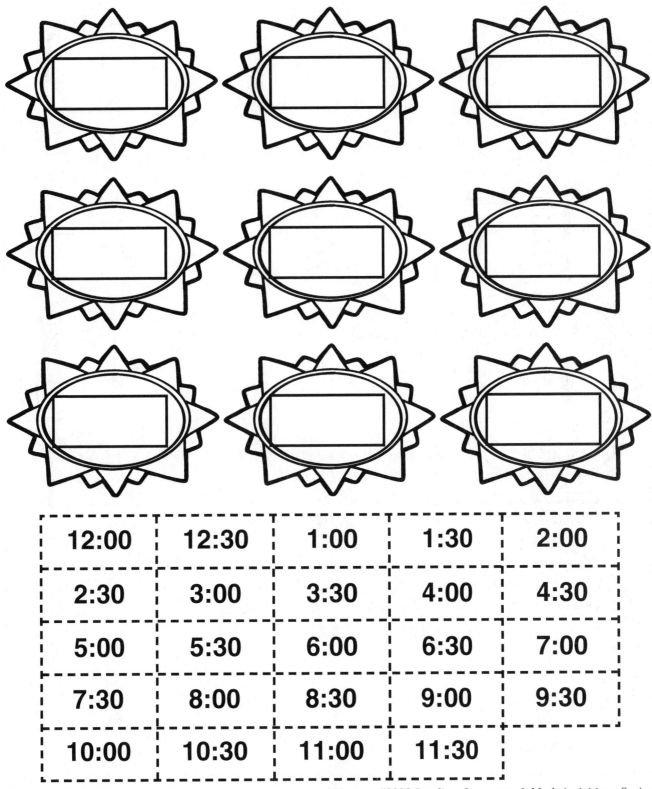

12:00	12:30	1:00	1:30	2:00
2:30	3:00	3:30	4:00	4:30
5:00	5:30	6:00	6:30	7:00
7:30	8:00	8:30	9:00	9:30
10:00	10:30	11:00	11:30	

Paper Bag Kites

Directions

Make your own paper bag kite and watch it fly off into the sky!

1. Take one paper lunch sack (any size will do).

2. Cut the bottom off of the bag.

3. Open the bag so that it will stand up on the table.

4. Fold down the top edges about 2" all around the bag.

5. Take a piece of masking tape and tape next to the fold on one of the long sides of the bag.

6. Using a hole punch, punch a hole in the masking tape.

7. Take a length of kite string. Tape one end of the string to a craft stick. Wind the remaining length of string around the craft stick. Tie the other end of the string through the hole in the paper sack.

8. Turn the bag over. Use glue to attach 6-8 pieces of tissue paper (approximately 2" x 12") to the inside of the paper bag (on all sides). Let the glue dry.

9. Wait for a windy day and take the kites outside and let them fly!

Answer Key

Page 93

Facts

    Kites need wind to fly.

    Kites have a tail.

    A kite's frame can be covered with paper, fabric, or plastic.

Opinions

    Kites are fun to fly.

    Kites are pretty.

    Only kids can fly kites.

Sample sentence: Kites can come in many different shapes.

Page 94

Cold Days	Hot Days
build a snowman	go swimming
go skiing	wear shorts
wear a jacket	play baseball

Sample sentence: During the summer, it is hot.

Page 95

1. box kite
2. frame
3. kite
4. string
5. tail
6. box kite
7. frame
8. string
9. tail
10. kite

Page 99

Page 100

Page 101

Page 102

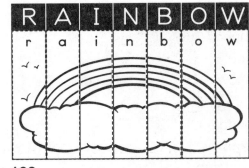

Page 108

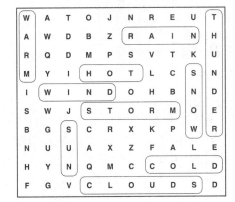

Page 109

C	L	O	U	D	B	U	R	S	T
A	G	I	S	O	A	H	R	D	S
Q	E	Z	H	W	Z	H	L	R	T
S	N	C	O	N	U	A	I	I	O
L	T	J	W	P	K	I	Z	Z	R
E	L	B	E	O	F	L	W	Z	M
E	E	O	R	U	D	B	E	L	R
T	P	O	U	R	I	N	G	E	A
N	F	L	O	O	D	V	D	M	I
C	S	P	R	I	N	K	L	E	N

Answer Key

Page 110

Page 111

1. thunder
2. sun
3. snow
4. rain
5. lightning
6. cold

Page 115

1. puddles
2. rainbow
3. lightning
4. sun
5. thermometer
6. cloud

Page 116

1. cover
2. frame
3. reel
4. tail
5. line

Page 125

1. January 1
2. April 1
3. fools
4. fake invitations

Page 126

1. 7
2. water and sunlight
3. full circle
4. black

Page 127

1. square
2. dragon
3. diamond
4. cartoon

	square kite	cartoon kite	diamond kite	dragon kite
Andrea	O	X	X	X
Joey	X	X	X	O
Noreen	X	X	O	X
Trevor	X	O	X	X

Page 128

Kite #4

Sample clue: The kite is plain.

Page 129

1. 4, 5, 9
2. 3
3. 1
4. 2
5. dragon kite

Page 130

1. sunny
2. snowy
3. sunny
4. Answers will vary.

Page 131

1. Wednesday
2. Friday
3. Tuesday
4. 5
5. 6
6. 27

Page 132

1. 90°
2. 20°
3. 50°
4. 60°
5. 80°
6. 10°
7. 30°
8. 70°
9. 40°

Page 133

1.
2.
3.

4.
5.
6.

7.
8.
9.

Answer Key

Page 134

1. Circle picture of swimmer.

2. Circle picture of playground or tricycling.

3. Circle picture of fishing or baseball.

4. Circle picture of ice hockey.

5. Circle picture of the beach.

Page 135

1. Circle picture of mittens.

2. Circle picture of thongs or short overalls.

3. Circle picture of hiking boot.

4. Circle picture of pants or earmuffs.

5. Circle picture of sunglasses or t-shirt.

Page 136

The kite is worth 10¢.

Page 137

The kite is worth 18¢.

Page 138

The kite is worth 22¢.

Page 139

The kite is worth 23¢.

Page 140

Answers will vary.

Page 141

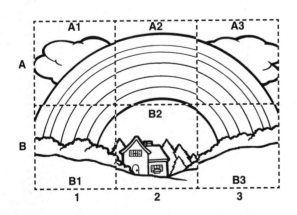

Page 142

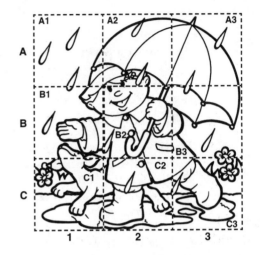

Page 143

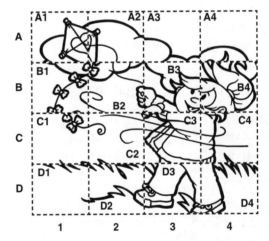

Page 144

1. 9 cm

2. 5 cm

3. 3 cm

4. 6 cm

5. 10 cm

Page 146

1. E1

2. sun

3. D5

4. rainbow

Mother's Day, Plants, Bugs, Memorial Day, and May Day

Table of Contents

Introduction

This section (Mother's Day, Plants, Bugs, Memorial Day, and May Day) contains activities to supplement the events and themes that happen during the month of May.

Reading and Language Activities

- **Don't "Bug" My Garden (page 164):** Simply photocopy the page and use this as the cover for each short unit. Or, photocopy the appropriate level of writing paper on pages 6–11 for each student and staple the cover to those pages to make a writing packet.

- **Check-Off List (page 10):** Use the blank list to keep track of each student's language and reading activity as it is completed.

- **May Writing Prompts (pages 165–166):** Writing prompts are provided for each one of the four domains. The writing prompts are a fun way for students to explore what they know about moms, plants, bugs, Memorial Day, and May Day.

- **Insects (page 167) and About Plants (page 168):** Students cut out the statements, sort and glue them into the appropriate category. Then students write another true statement about one of the items.

- **Don't Bug Me! (page 169), Flowers (page 170), and Nuts for Peanuts (page 171):** Students place seasonally-related vocabulary words in alphabetical order.

- **Mother's Day (page 172), George Washington Carver (page 173), and Plants (page 174):** Students learn different holiday and theme-related facts from these mini-books. The pages can be cut apart and then stapled together to make a mini-booklet.

- **Letter Matches (pages 175–178):** These cut-and-paste activities reinforce identifying and matching uppercase and lowercase letters. Students cut out the "puzzle pieces" at the bottom of the page and glue them in place under the matching uppercase letter. If done correctly, the letters will spell a word and a picture will be revealed.

- **Making Questions and Statements (pages 179–180):** This activity contains rebus-like pictures and high-frequency words. Students cut apart the words and pictures and arrange and rearrange the words and pictures to make different questions and statements. When doing this activity with the whole class, make an overhead transparency of the pages or use a photocopy machine to enlarge the words and pictures so that they can be easily seen by all of the students. Some sample sentences are as follows:

Using the Plant Words	Using the Bug Words
I can plant the seeds.	I see a ladybug.
I can dig the hole.	Can you see a fly?
Where are the seeds?	Where is the butterfly?
How can I dig a hole?	How can a butterfly fly?
Who put the seeds in a hole?	What is a flower?
Where can I go?	Who can color the dragonfly?
You can plant a tree.	I can color the fly.

Introduction

Reading and Language Activities *(cont.)*

- **How Many Words Can You Make? (pages 181–182):** Students cut apart the letter cards and arrange and rearrange the letters to make different words. When doing this activity with the whole class, make an overhead transparency of the page. Call on individual students to use the overhead to show the class a word they have made. This is also a great activity to send home as homework. Sample words that can be made are as follows:

Using the Letters in "dragonfly"

two letters: or, ad, on

three letters: ray, far, lay, nog, for, dog, log, rag, fly, lad, God, oar

four letters: drag, flay, flag, goal, golf, yard, lard, glad, flog, road, load, goad

five+ letters: dragon, glory

Using the Letters in "Mother's Day"

two letters: at, to, he, so, am, ad, an, as

three letters: day, her, sad, had, mad, yes, say, ray, may, hay

four letters: moth, yard, moat, sear, dear, tear, year, mode, moat, head, heat, seat

five+ letters: hearth, mother, heard, Morse, darts

- **Garden Delights (pages 183–184):** This rebus story activity uses pictures and high-frequency words to tell a story. Students feel successful when they are able to read the story with little or no help from the teacher!

The story reads as follows: *Jay and May found some seeds. Jay and May planted the seeds in the soil. Soon the seeds began to grow and grow. The seeds became beautiful flowers. Bees came to drink nectar from the flowers. Butterflies came to drink nectar from the flowers. Ladybugs came to eat bugs from the flowers. Jay and May picked the flowers and put them in a vase. Jay and May gave the flowers to Mom. Happy Mother's Day!*

- **Moms are #1! (page 185):** Students find vocabulary words about moms in a word search.

- **Bug Bingo (pages 186–188):** The bingo game includes eight different bingo cards and matching calling cards. The bingo game reinforces bug-related vocabulary and language development skills in a fun-filled, non-threatening manner.

- **George Washington Carver (page 189):** This activity has students identifying the peanut-related products he or she has used or knows. Student then write a sentence about one of their favorite products.

- **Parts of a Plant (page 190), Bugs (page 191), Parts of a Rose Bush (page 192), and Parts of an Ant (page 193):** In these activities, students place labels underneath a picture or write the words on a diagram.

- **Jack and the Beanstalk (page 194):** This is a sequencing activity. Students cut out the sentence strips, read each strip, and place them in the correct order on a clean sheet of paper.

- **Homonyms (pages 195–210):** This activity introduces the concept of homonyms (homophones) to students in a concrete manner through a variety of games and pocket chart activities.

- **Memorial Day (page 211) and May Day (page 212):** These two pages provide students with basic information on these two topics, as well as a few questions for students to answer about what they have just read.

Introduction

Math Activities

- **How Do the Gardens Grow? (page 213), Which One is Mom's Favorite? (page 214) and Who Ate the Plant? (page 215):** These are logic activities. As each clue is read, students cross off the pictures that meet (or do not meet) the clue.

- **Gifts for Mom (page 216):** Students read and answer questions about a chart.

- **Flags Sold (page 217):** Students read and answer questions about a chart.

- **Peanuts (page 218):** Students construct a graph based on ten classmates' favorite ways to eat peanuts. Students answer questions about the graph they created.

- **Time (pages 219–221):** Students are introduced to the quarter past and quarter 'til aspects of time.

- **Quarters (pages 222–223):** Students practice counting coins to make 25¢, as well as draw specific coins to make 25¢.

- **Plant Power (page 224):** Students cut out the ruler at the bottom of the page and measure plants to the nearest inch.

- **May Calendar (page 225):** Students put together all the different parts of a calendar onto a blank calendar (page 64) and then answer some questions about it.

- **Remembering (page 226), A Butterfly's Life (page 227), and Mom's Day (page 228):** Students glue all the pieces of the puzzle in the correct place on the graph to form a picture.

- **Where's Jack? (page 229):** Students use directional words to locate "Jack" on the map.

- **Ladybug Sorting (pages 230–231):** This activity can be done with the whole class. Make an overhead transparency of both pages. Place the large cloud on the overhead projector. Place several of pictures inside the large shape and the remaining pictures outside the shape. Ask the students, "What is the rule to be in this family?" Call on students to answer. Suggested ways to sort the ladybug pictures are as follows:

  > Number of spots
  >
  > Those with spots/without spots
  >
  > Number of legs showing
  >
  > Those with faces
  >
  > Those sitting down/standing/flying
  >
  > Color of spots

- **Bug Patterns (pages 232–233):** Students make patterns using theme-related pictures. Photocopy the pattern sleeve onto construction paper, fold and glue in the back to create the sleeve. For each student, provide three to four 12" lengths of sentence strips. Photocopy a class set of theme-related pictures. Have students cut out the pictures and use the pictures to make different patterns on the sentence strips.

- **Get to the Hive! (pages 234–237):** This is a game the reinforces place value (tens and ones), numbers, number words, and expanded notation.

Don't "Bug" My Garden

May Writing Prompts

Domain	Writing Prompt	Word Bank
Practical/Informative	Honoring Veterans	country, flags, flowers, fought, freedom, parades, remembering, soldiers, war
Practical/Informative	How to Grow a Beanstalk	climb, giant, high, magic, plant, seed, sky, soil, sunlight, tall, water, yard
Practical/Informative	Ten Things a Mom Does Best	With the students, brainstorm a list of things that Moms do best.
Practical/Informative	How to Make Peanut Butter	bag, bowl, collect, crack, crush, jar, lid, mash, open, shells, spoon, squish, stir
Analytical/Expository	What Makes My Mother So Special	cares, helps me, hugs, loves me, plays games, reads stories, takes care of me
Analytical/Expository	Should Jack have traded the cow for the beans?	With the students, brainstorm good and bad reasons for trading the cow for beans.
Analytical/Expository	If you were a seed, which one would you be and why?	With the students, brainstorm a list of different plant seeds and the positives associated with the seed.
Analytical/Expository	Do plants have feelings?	With the students, brainstorm a list of reasons why a plant may or may not have feelings.

May Writing Prompts

Domain	Writing Prompt	Word Bank
Imaginative/Narrative	Pretend you climbed a beanstalk. What would you find when you reached the top?	With the students, brainstorm a list of possible outcomes.
Imaginative/Narrative	You discover a new bug. Tell everything about it.	antennas, beautiful, colors, dots, furry, large, rough, small, soft, strange, wings
Imaginative/Narrative	Retell *The Very Hungry Caterpillar* with a different ending.	ate through, butterfly, caterpillar, changed, cocoon, food, fruits, vegetables
Imaginative/Narrative	Pretend you traded lives with your mom. Tell about your day.	breakfast, clean, cook, homework, hugs, kids, lunches, stories, wake up, work
Sensory/Descriptive	Describe how a butterfly would feel.	bumpy, delicate, fluttery, light, scales, smooth, soft, thin, tickles
Sensory/Descriptive	Describe your favorite bug.	abdomen, antennas, eyes, flies, hard, hops, jumps, legs, shell, soft, thorax, wings
Sensory/Descriptive	How do plants smell?	blossoms, centers, flower, leaves, petals, roots, stems, trunks
Sensory/Descriptive	Describe your mom.	best, curly, good, hair, long, old, short, smells, soft, straight, tall, young

Insects

Directions: Cut out and glue each statement under the correct category.

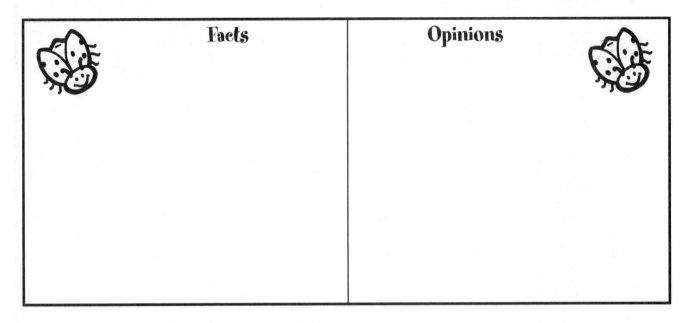

Facts	Opinions

Directions: Write another true statement about insects.

_____

- -

_____

_____

- -

_____

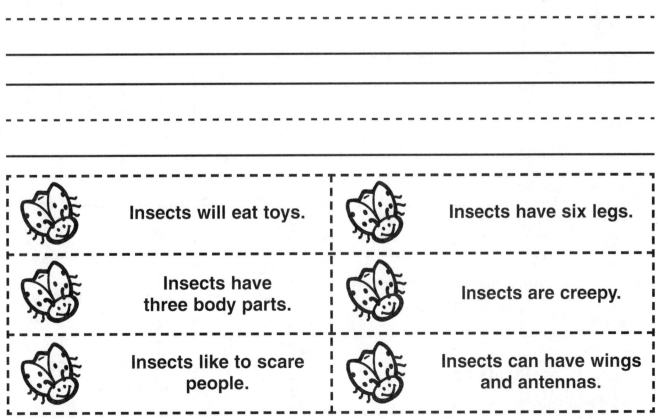

Insects will eat toys.	Insects have six legs.
Insects have three body parts.	Insects are creepy.
Insects like to scare people.	Insects can have wings and antennas.

About Plants

Directions: Cut out the boxes at the bottom of the page. Then glue them under the correct category.

True Statements	False Statements

Directions: Write another true statement about plants.

_____

- -

_____

_____

- -

_____

Plants grow in soil.		Plants are related to people.
There are many different kinds of plants.		Plants grow in the sky.
Plants have bones.		Plants have stems and roots.

Don't Bug Me!

Directions: Cut out the words at the bottom of the page. Put the words in alphabetical order and then answer each question.

1.	
2.	
3.	
4.	
5.	

6. Which word is <u>first</u>?

_____

7. Which word comes <u>after</u> *dragonfly*?

_____

8. Which word comes <u>before</u> *dragonfly*?

_____

9. Which word is <u>last</u>?

_____

10. Which word is in <u>between</u> *butterfly* and *grasshopper*?

_____

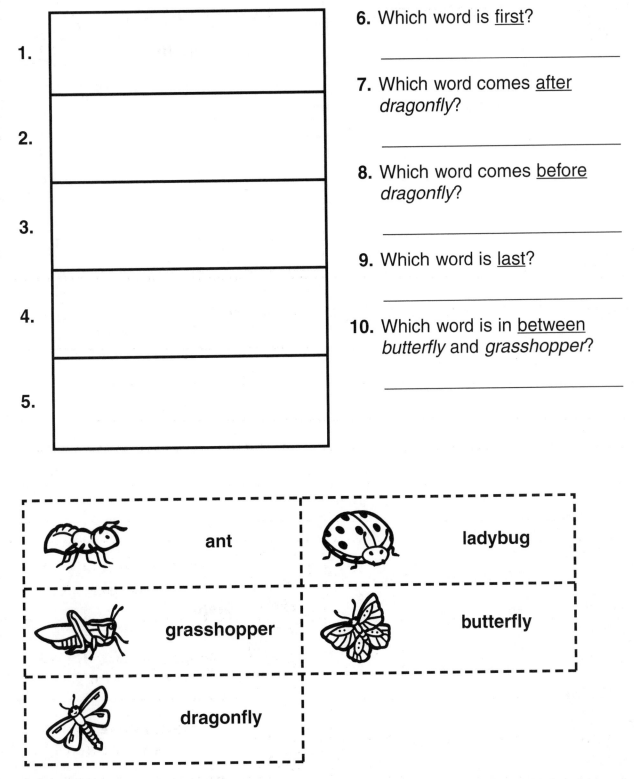

ant

ladybug

grasshopper

butterfly

dragonfly

Flowers

Directions: Cut out the words at the bottom of the page. Put the words in alphabetical order and then answer each question.

1. _____
2. _____
3. _____
4. _____
5. _____

6. Which word is <u>first</u>?

   _____

7. Which word comes <u>after</u> *daisy*?

   _____

8. Which word comes <u>before</u> *tulip*?

   _____

9. Which word is <u>last</u>?

   _____

10. Which word is in <u>between</u> *poinsettia* and *sunflower*?

    _____

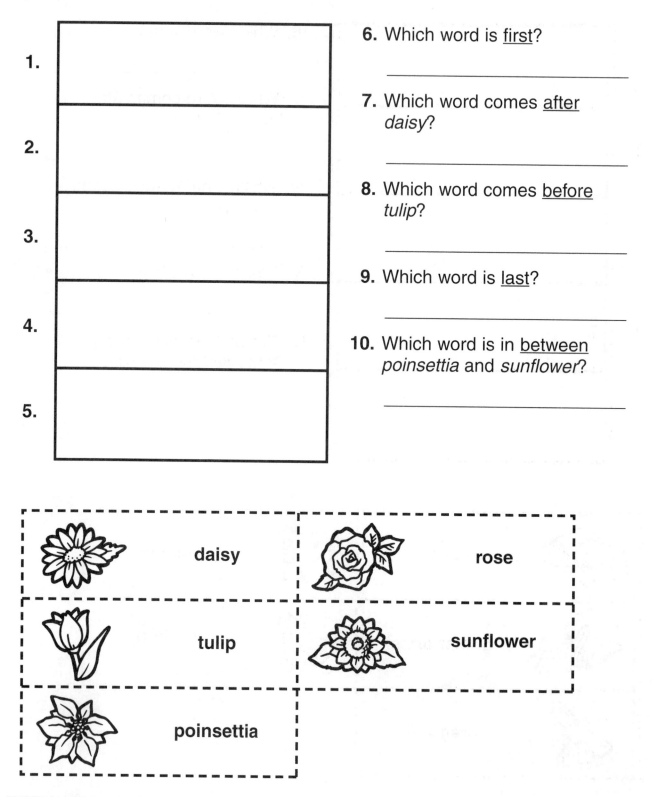

daisy

rose

tulip

sunflower

poinsettia

Nuts for Peanuts

Directions: Cut out the words at the bottom of the page. Put the words in alphabetical order and then answer each question.

1.	
2.	
3.	
4.	
5.	

6. Which word is <u>first</u>?

_____

7. Which word comes <u>after</u> *fudge*?

_____

8. Which word comes <u>before</u> *milk*?

_____

9. Which word is <u>last</u>?

_____

10. Which word is in <u>between</u> *butter* and *fudge*?

_____

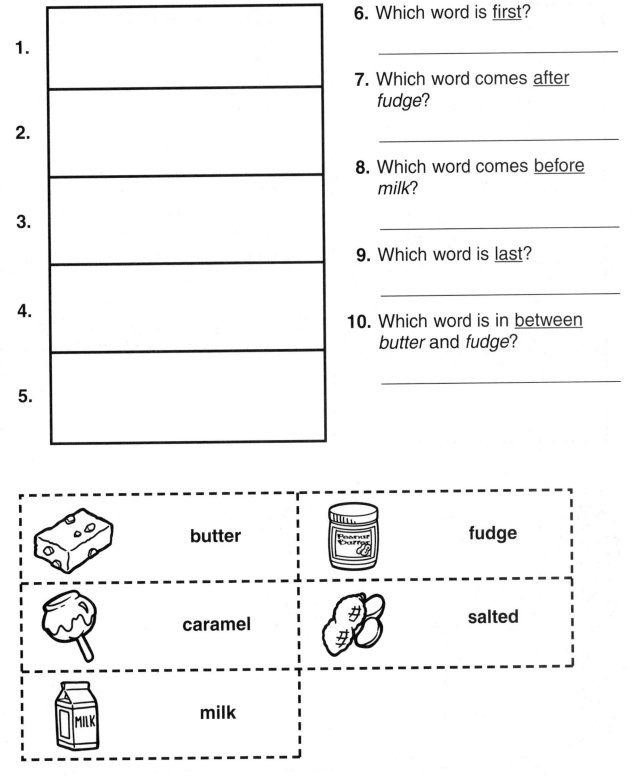

butter

fudge

caramel

salted

milk

3 In 1907, Anna Jarvis wanted Mother's Day to be a national holiday.

6 Mother's Day is the second Sunday in May.

2 In 1872, Julia Ward Howe suggested Mother's Day.

5 In 1914, President Wilson made it a national holiday.

1 Mother's Day

Name: _____

4 In 1911, almost every state celebrates Mother's Day.

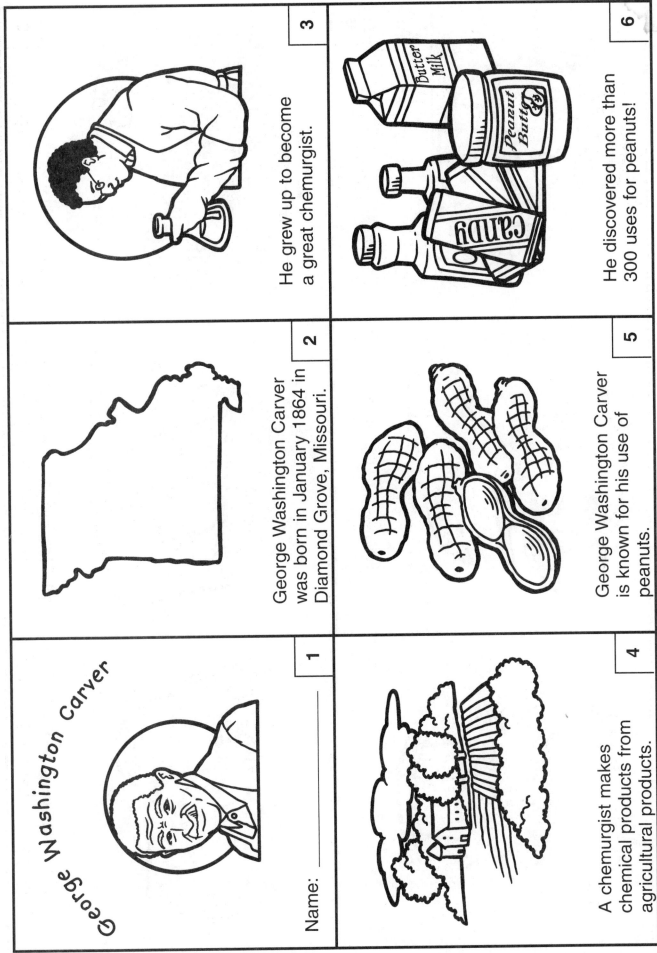

3

He grew up to become a great chemurgist.

6

He discovered more than 300 uses for peanuts!

2

George Washington Carver was born in January 1864 in Diamond Grove, Missouri.

5

George Washington Carver is known for his use of peanuts.

George Washington Carver

1

Name: _____

4

A chemurgist makes chemical products from agricultural products.

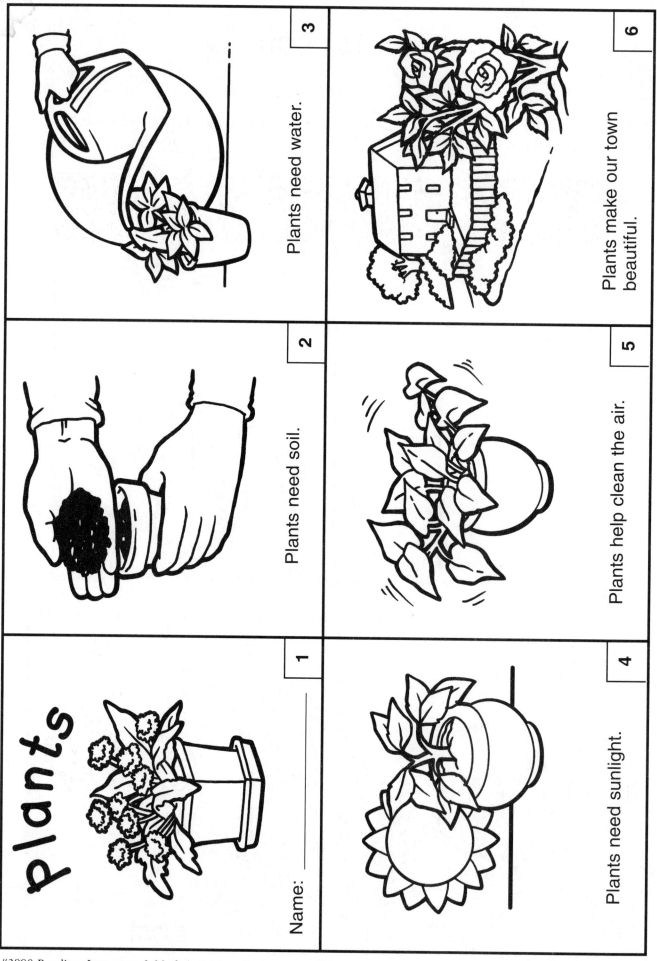

3

Plants need water.

6

Plants make our town beautiful.

2

Plants need soil.

5

Plants help clean the air.

Plants

1

Name: _____

4

Plants need sunlight.

Letter Match

Directions: Cut out the boxes at the bottom of the page. Glue the lowercase letter box to the uppercase letter box to find a picture.

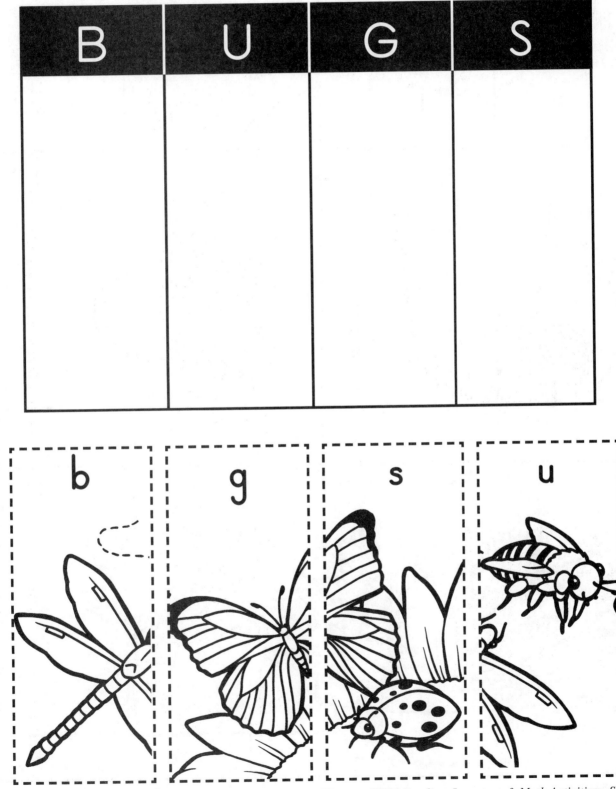

B	U	G	S

b   g   s   u

Letter Match

Directions: Cut out the boxes at the bottom of the page. Glue the lowercase letter box to the uppercase letter box to find a picture.

P	L	A	N	T

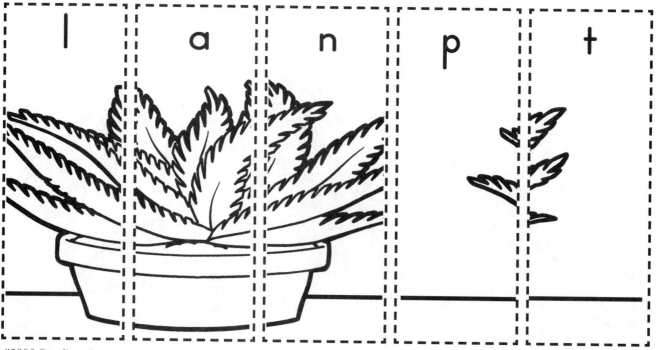

l   a   n   p   t

Letter Match

Directions: Cut out the boxes at the bottom of the page. Glue the lowercase letter box to the uppercase letter box to find a picture.

M	O	T	H	E	R

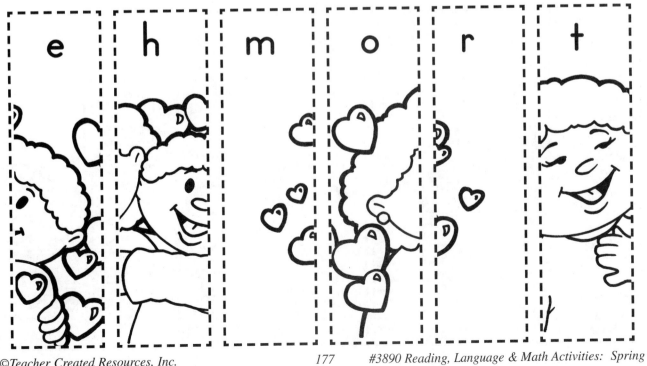

e	h	m	o	r	t

Letter Match

Directions: Cut out the boxes at the bottom of the page. Glue the lowercase letter box to the uppercase letter box to find a picture.

M	A	Y	P	O	L	E

a   e   l   m   o   p   y

Making Questions and Statements

Directions: Cut apart the picture and word cards. Arrange and rearrange the cards to make different questions and statements.

seeds	plant	dig
hole	tree	water
Did	can	I
What	the	the
go	you	How
put	in	a
Where	are	do
Who	.	?

Making Questions and Statements

Directions: Cut apart the picture and word cards. Arrange and rearrange the cards to make different questions and statements.

ladybug	flower	bee
dragonfly	fly	leaf
butterfly	can	I
	the	see
	you	a
the	is	What
Who	on	Where
How	.	?

How Many Words Can You Make?

Directions: Cut out the letters at the bottom of the page. Rearrange the letters to make different words. Write each word under the correct heading.

Two-Letter Words

Three-Letter Words

Four-Letter Words

Five-or-More-Letter Words

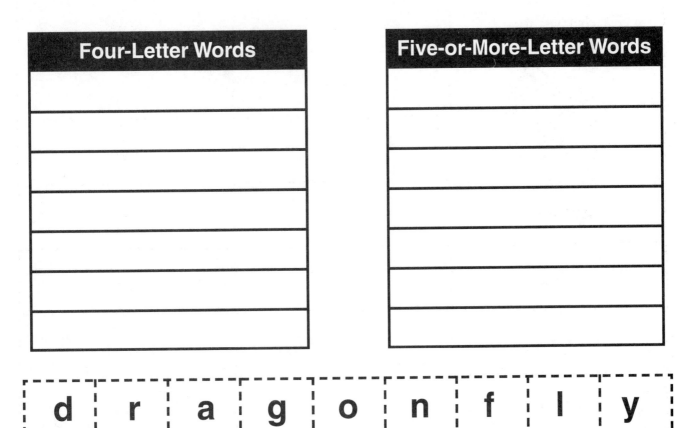

d r a g o n f l y

How Many Words Can You Make?

Directions: Cut out the letters at the bottom of the page. Rearrange the letters to make different words. Write each word under the correct heading.

Two-Letter Words

Three-Letter Words

Four-Letter Words

Five-or-More-Letter Words

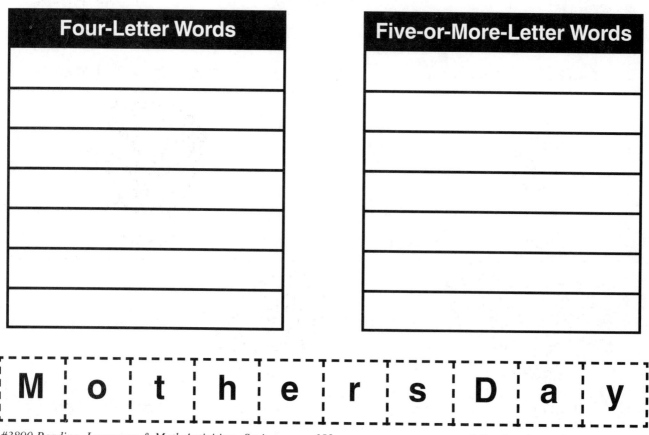

M o t h e r s D a y

Garden Delights

Jay   and   May   found   some seeds.   Jay   and   May

planted   the   seeds   in   the   soil.   Soon   the

seeds   began   to   grow   and   grow.

The   seeds   became   beautiful   flowers.

Bees   came   to   drink   nectar   from

Garden Delights

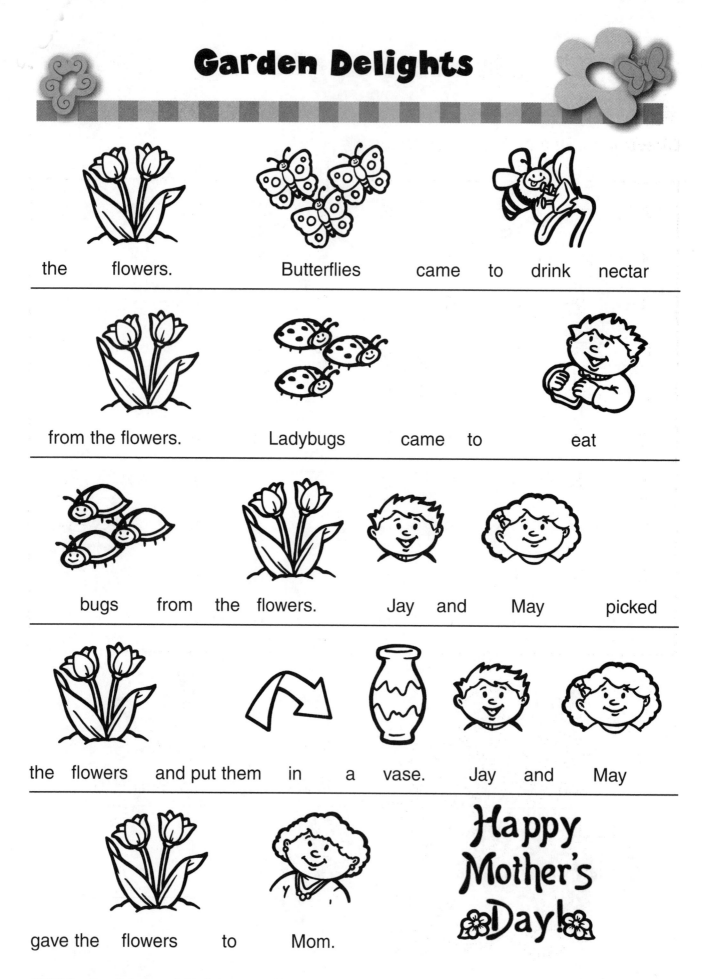

the   flowers.   Butterflies   came   to   drink   nectar

from the flowers.   Ladybugs   came   to   eat

bugs   from   the   flowers.   Jay   and   May   picked

the   flowers   and put them   in   a   vase.   Jay   and   May

gave the   flowers   to   Mom.

Moms are #1!

Directions: Find and color each word.

```
A   L   K   W   R   E   A   D   S   K
X   O   S   A   L   H   P   H   W   I
J   V   K   R   B   B   V   C   O   S
N   E   G   M   R   R   T   G   O   S
F   Q   V   M   O   T   H   E   R   E
C   Q   X   Z   U   F   N   J   U   S
A   A   E   D   S   A   F   E   A   I
R   W   Y   P   H   E   L   P   S   M
E   H   O   M   E   M   Z   D   I   S
S   E   T   L   H   U   G   S   Y   C
```

CARES   LOVE

HELPS   MOTHER

HOME   READS

HUGS   SAFE

KISSES   WARM

Bug Bingo

Directions: Photocopy the calling cards below onto cardstock, color, laminate, and cut apart. Provide each student with a game board (pages 187 and 188) and some counters (beans, pennies, multilinks, etc.). Mix up the calling cards. As each card is read aloud, have students cover the matching picture on their boards with a counter. The first student to get three in a row (vertically, horizontally, or diagonally) wins the game.

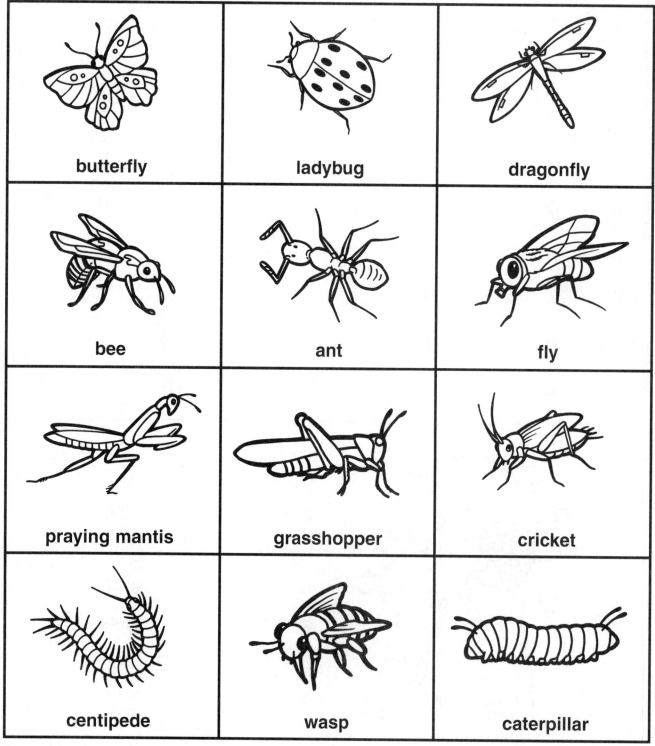

butterfly	ladybug	dragonfly
bee	ant	fly
praying mantis	grasshopper	cricket
centipede	wasp	caterpillar

Bug Bingo

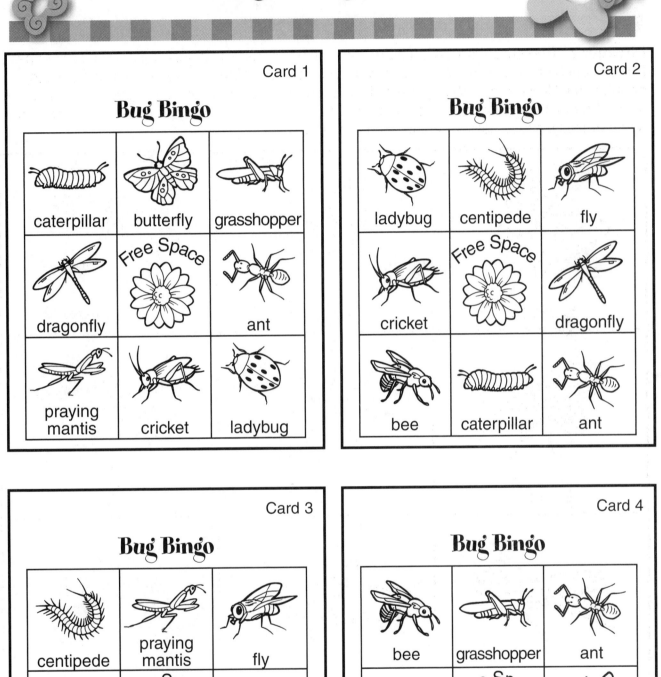

Card 1

Bug Bingo

caterpillar	butterfly	grasshopper
dragonfly	Free Space	ant
praying mantis	cricket	ladybug

Card 2

Bug Bingo

ladybug	centipede	fly
cricket	Free Space	dragonfly
bee	caterpillar	ant

Card 3

Bug Bingo

centipede	praying mantis	fly
ladybug	Free Space	bee
butterfly	caterpillar	cricket

Card 4

Bug Bingo

bee	grasshopper	ant
wasp	Free Space	butterfly
fly	dragonfly	centipede

Bug Bingo

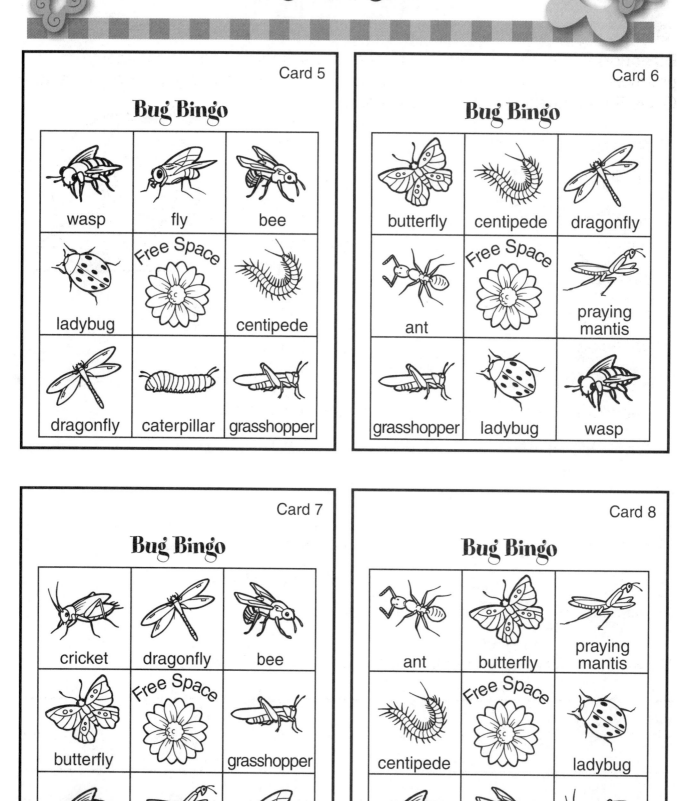

Card 5

Bug Bingo

wasp	fly	bee
ladybug	Free Space	centipede
dragonfly	caterpillar	grasshopper

Card 6

Bug Bingo

butterfly	centipede	dragonfly
ant	Free Space	praying mantis
grasshopper	ladybug	wasp

Card 7

Bug Bingo

cricket	dragonfly	bee
butterfly	Free Space	grasshopper
wasp	praying mantis	fly

Card 8

Bug Bingo

ant	butterfly	praying mantis
centipede	Free Space	ladybug
wasp	bee	cricket

George Washington Carver

Directions: George Washington Carver is well known for inventing many products made from peanuts. Below are some of the products that he invented. Circle the products that you have used.

bar candy	mayonnaise
breakfast foods	pancake flour
buttermilk	peanut bar
butter	peanut brittle
caramel	peanut cake
cream cheese	peanut chocolate fudge
cheese sandwich	peanut flakes
chili sauce	peanut kisses
chocolate coated peanuts	peanut sausage
chop suey sauce	peanut wafers
cocoa	pickle
cream candy	salad oil
crystallized peanuts	salted peanuts
coffee	shredded peanuts
golden nuts	vinegar

Directions: Write a sentence about your favorite peanut product.

_____

- -

_____

_____

- -

_____

Parts of a Plant

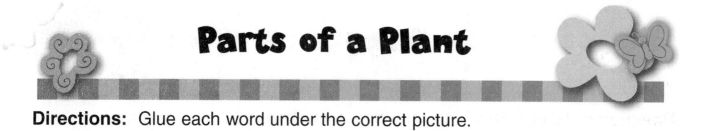

Directions: Glue each word under the correct picture.

1.	2.	3.

4.	5.	6.

branch	seeds
leaf	sprout
roots	trunk

Bugs

Directions: Glue each word under the correct picture.

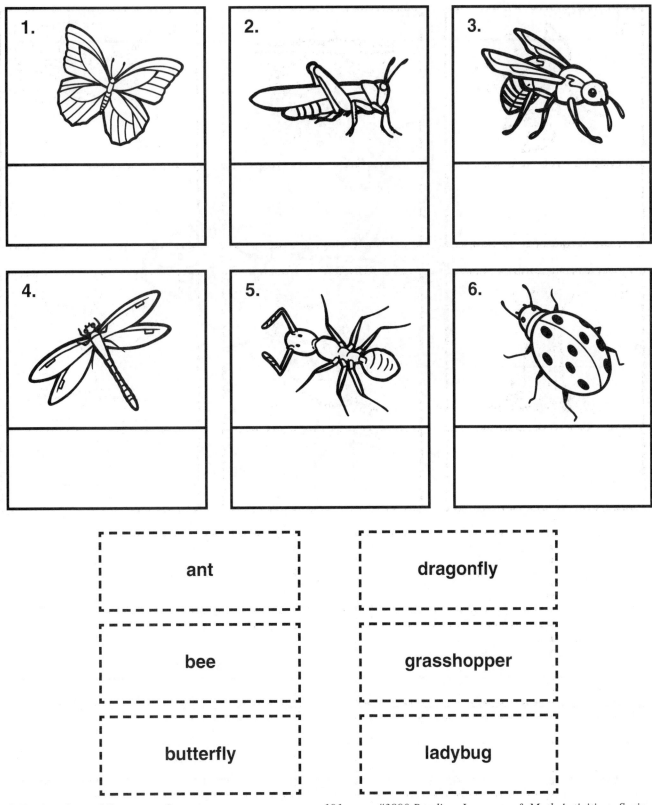

1.

2.

3.

4.

5.

6.

ant

dragonfly

bee

grasshopper

butterfly

ladybug

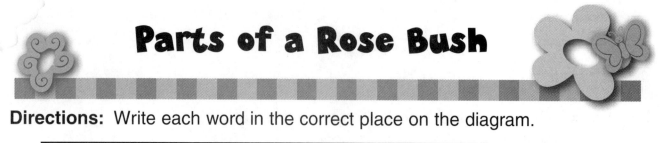

Parts of a Rose Bush

Directions: Write each word in the correct place on the diagram.

blossom	branch	leaf	roots	trunk

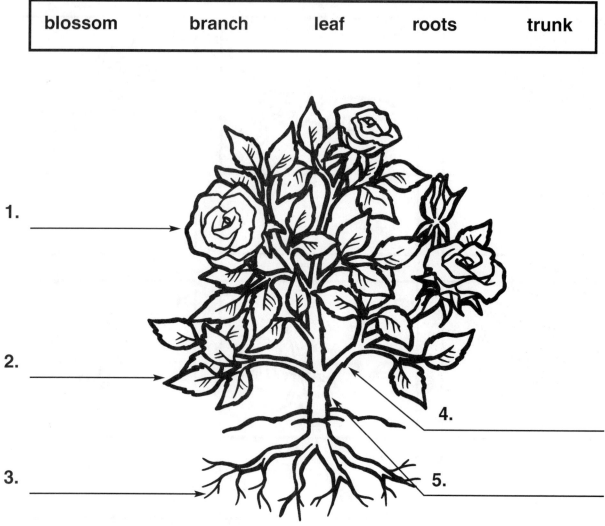

1. _____

2. _____

3. _____

4. _____

5. _____

Directions: Write a sentence about the picture.

_____

- -

_____

_____

- -

_____

Parts of an Ant

Directions: Write each word in the correct place on the diagram.

abdomen	antenna	head	leg	thorax

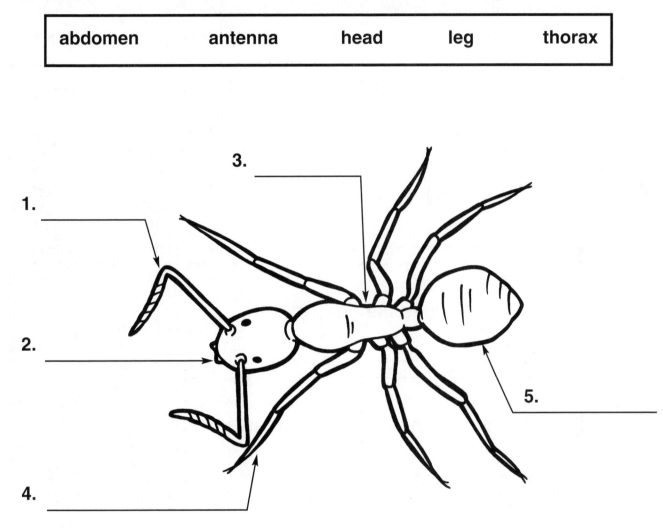

Directions: Write a sentence about the picture.

_____

- -

_____

_____

- -

_____

Jack and the Beanstalk

Directions: Cut out the statements below. Glue the statements in the correct order on a separate sheet of paper.

Jack stole the hen that lays golden eggs.

Jack and his mom never went hungry again.

Jack climbed the beanstalk.

Jack sold the cow for five magic beans.

Jack chopped down the beanstalk.

The Giant chased Jack down the beanstalk.

The beanstalk grew and grew.

Homonyms

Homonyms (or *homophones*) are two words that sound the same but have different meanings and spellings. The following activities introduce homonyms in a concrete manner to young students.

Homonym Picture and Word Cards (pages 196–199) Photocopy, color, laminate, and cut apart the cards. Introduce the homonym pairs to the students and ask the students to use each word correctly in a sentence.

- Play Concentration: Shuffle the cards and lay them out face-down in a 4 x 6 arrangement. Taking turns, each player turns over two cards. If the cards are homonym pairs, the player keeps both cards and takes another turn. If the cards are not homonym pairs, the student returns the cards to their original places and play continues with the next player. The player with the most pairs wins the game.

- Extension Activity: Brainstorm a list of other homonyms. This list can be used by students when working on their writing journals.

- Extension Activity: Have students make new homonym cards. Provide each student with two pieces of 4" x 4" white paper. Have each student write a homonym on each piece of paper (Example—sum, some). Have the student illustrate each homonym. The completed homonym cards can be displayed on a bulletin board.

Homonym Picture Cards (pages 200–201) and Land of the Homonyms (page 202) Photocopy, color, laminate, and cut apart the picture cards and one playing board for each small group of students. Provide each group of students with tokens (multilinks, coins, small items of different colors, etc.). Have students place their tokens in the start box. Taking turns, each player turns over a picture card, identifies the homonym, and moves his or her token to the nearest matching pair of homonym words. The first player to reach the castle wins the game.

- Extension Activity (Matching): Students match the homonym pairs.

- Extension Activity: Students use both words in one sentence or separate sentences. (Examples: I have a pair of pears. I have a green pear. I have a new pair of shoes.)

Homonym Sentence Strips for the Pocket Chart (pages 203–210) and Homonym Picture and Word Cards (pages 196–199) or Homonym Picture Cards (pages 200–201) This is a great activity for the pocket chart. Photocopy and cut apart the sentences. Place the sentences in a pocket chart. Provide each student with a set of picture and word cards or a set of picture cards. Students read each sentence and complete each sentence with the appropriate homonym card. The answers for the homonym sentences are as follows:

I <u>blew</u> out the candle.	The jeans are <u>blue</u>.	The man will <u>buy</u> the map.
The kids said <u>bye</u>.	Do you see the <u>pear</u>?	Bob has a new <u>pair</u> of shoes.
Who has the <u>right</u> answer?	I can <u>write</u> the note.	Who <u>ate</u> the cake?
An octopus has <u>eight</u> legs.	An <u>ant</u> can be black or red.	My <u>aunt</u> is a vet.
My <u>son</u> likes baseball.	Is the <u>sun</u> in the sky?	The gift is <u>for</u> you!
A dog has <u>four</u> legs.	An apple is <u>red</u>.	Mom <u>read</u> the book to us.
I have <u>one</u> cat.	Who <u>won</u> the game?	Don't step on my <u>toe</u>!
Did you call the <u>tow</u> truck?	I have <u>eye</u> glasses.	<u>I</u> go to school.

Homonyms

blew

blue

buy

bye

pear

pair

Homonyms

right

write

ate

eight

ant

aunt

Homonyms

son

sun

for

four

red

read

Homonyms

one

won

toe

tow

eye

I

Homonyms

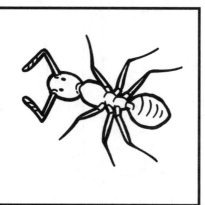

Homonyms

 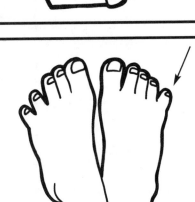

Land of the Homonyms

Start →	son / sun	toe / tow	eye / I	right / write	blew / blue
one / won	blew / blue	ant / aunt	eye / I	for / four	ate / eight
right / write					pear / pair
ate / eight	for / four	read / red	one / won	bye / buy	

Directions (for 2–4 players): Each student places his or her marker on "Start." Taking turns, each player turns over one of the homonym picture cards (without the word), identifies the homonym, and moves his or her marker to the nearest matching pair of homonyms. If another player lands in the same place, the first player gets bumped back to Start. The first player to reach the castle wins the game.

Homonyms

Directions: Photocopy the sentence strips in the pocket chart. Have students read each sentence and then complete the sentence with the appropriate homonym picture and word card.

 I _____ out the candle.

The jeans are _____.

The man will _____ the map.

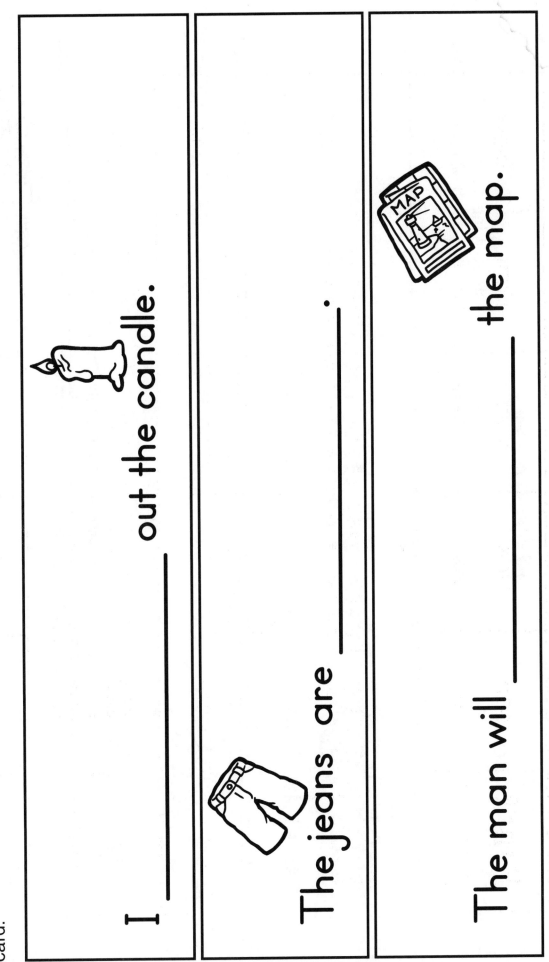

Homonyms

Directions: Photocopy the sentence strips and cut apart. Place the sentence strips in the pocket chart. Have students read each sentence and then complete the sentence with the appropriate homonym picture and word card.

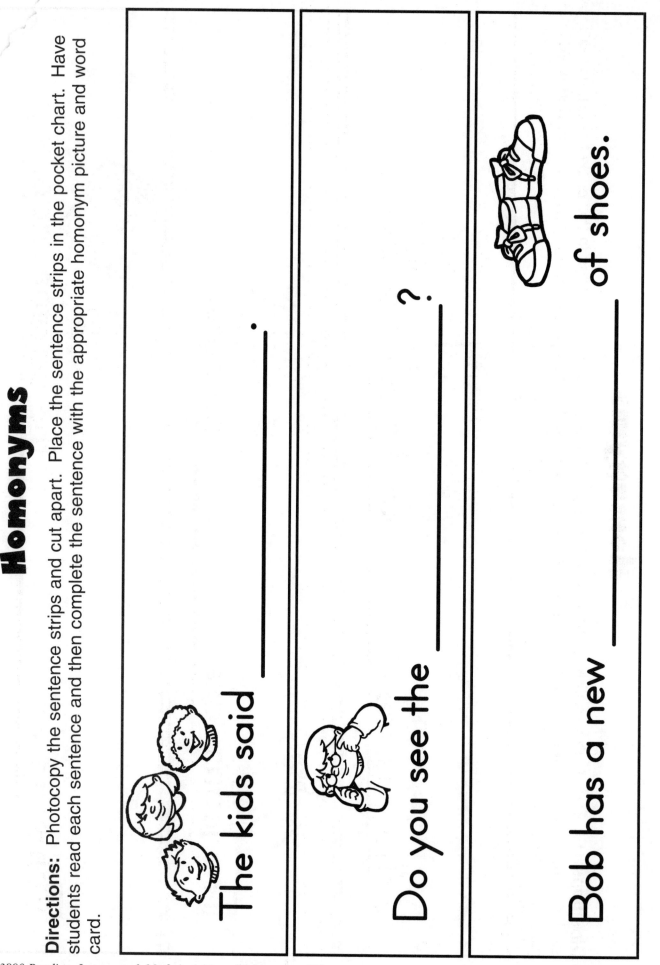

The kids said _____.

Do you see the _____?

Bob has a new _____ of shoes.

Homonyms

Directions: Photocopy the sentence strips and cut apart. Place the sentence strips in the pocket chart. Have students read each sentence and then complete the sentence with the appropriate homonym picture and word card.

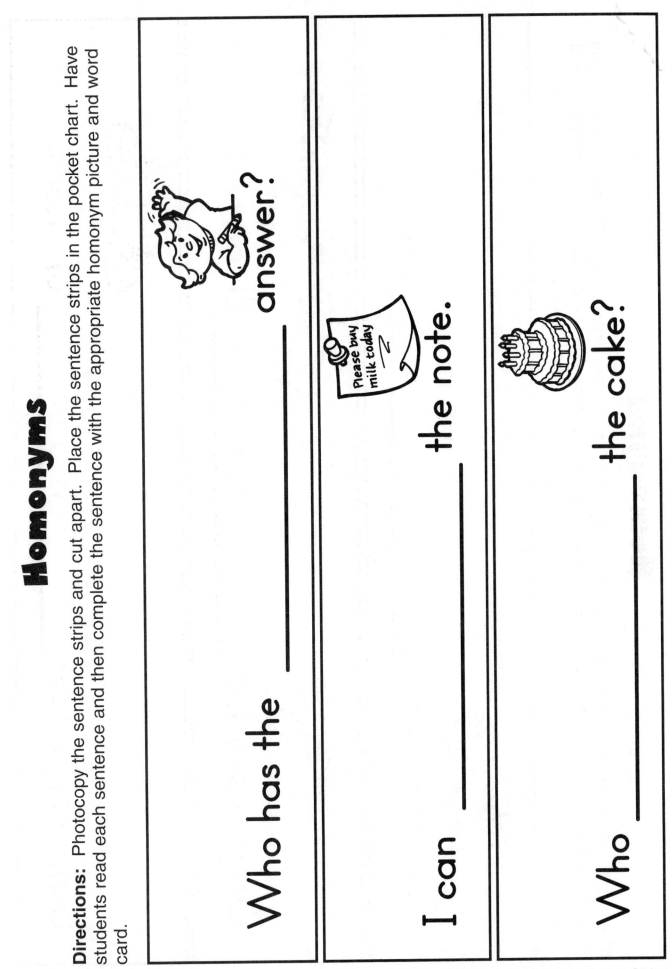

Who has the _____ answer?

I can _____ the note.

Who _____ the cake?

Homonyms

Directions: Photocopy the sentence strips and cut apart. Place the sentence strips in the pocket chart. Have students read each sentence and then complete the sentence with the appropriate homonym picture and word card.

An octopus has _____ legs.

An _____ can be black or red.

My _____ is a vet.

Homonyms

Directions: Photocopy the sentence strips and cut apart. Place the sentence strips in the pocket chart. Have students read each sentence and then complete the sentence with the appropriate homonym picture and word card.

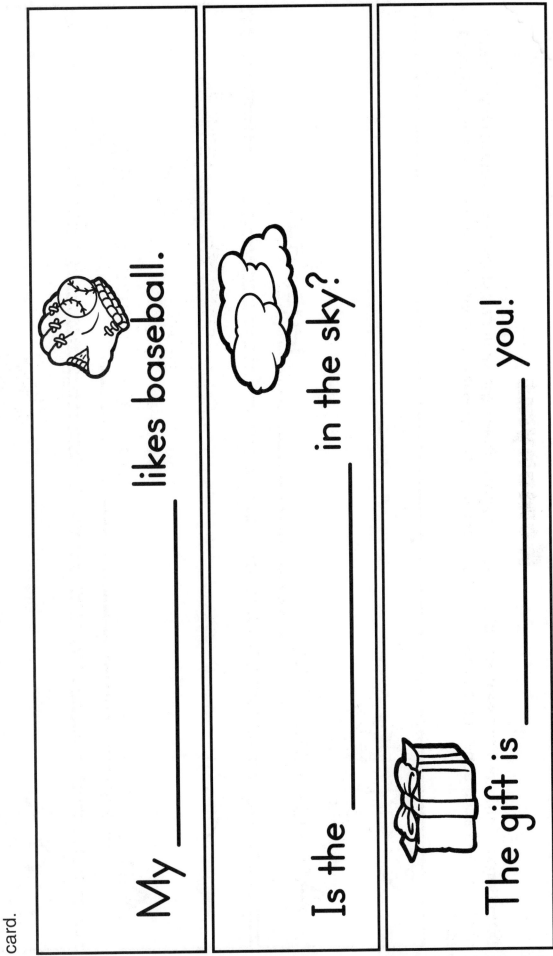

My _____ likes baseball.

Is the _____ in the sky?

The gift is _____ you!

Homonyms

Directions: Photocopy the sentence strips and cut apart. Place the sentence strips in the pocket chart. Have students read each sentence and then complete the sentence with the appropriate homonym picture and word card.

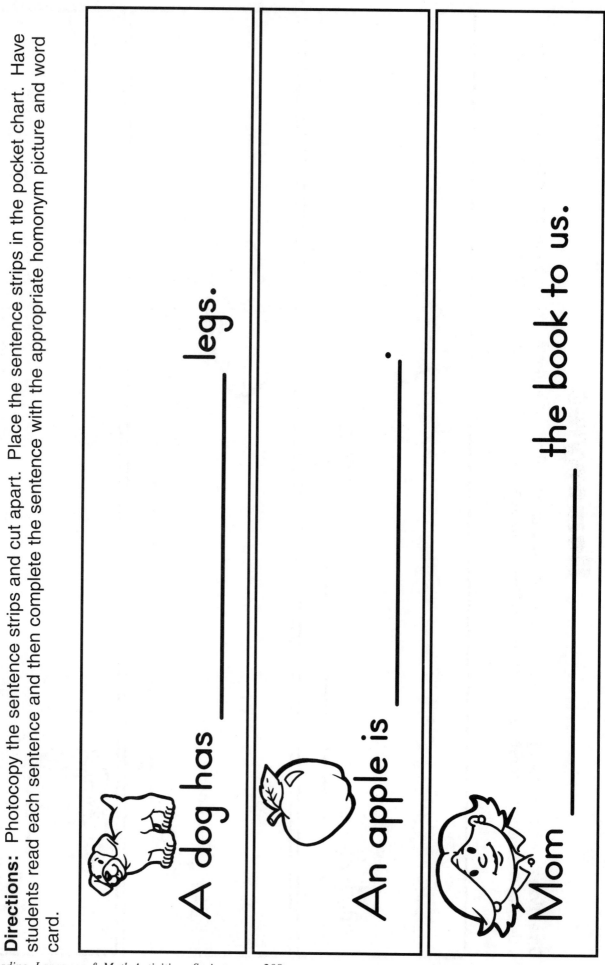

A dog has _____ legs.

An apple is _____.

Mom _____ the book to us.

Homonyms

Directions: Photocopy the sentence strips and cut apart. Place the sentence strips in the pocket chart. Have students read each sentence and then complete the sentence with the appropriate homonym picture and word card.

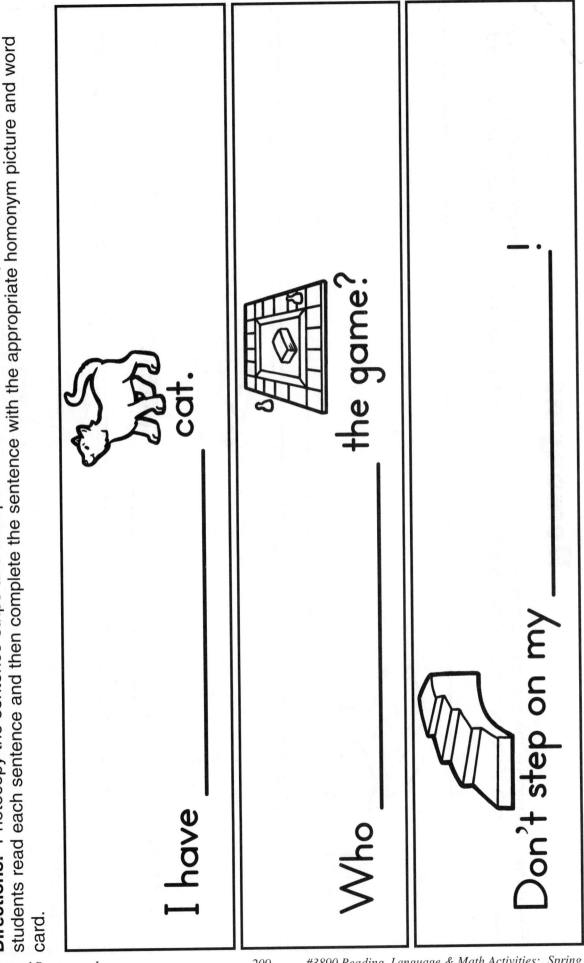

I have _____ cat.

Who _____ the game?

Don't step on my _____ !

Homonyms

Directions: Photocopy the sentence strips and cut apart. Place the sentence strips in the pocket chart. Have students read each sentence and then complete the sentence with the appropriate homonym picture and word card.

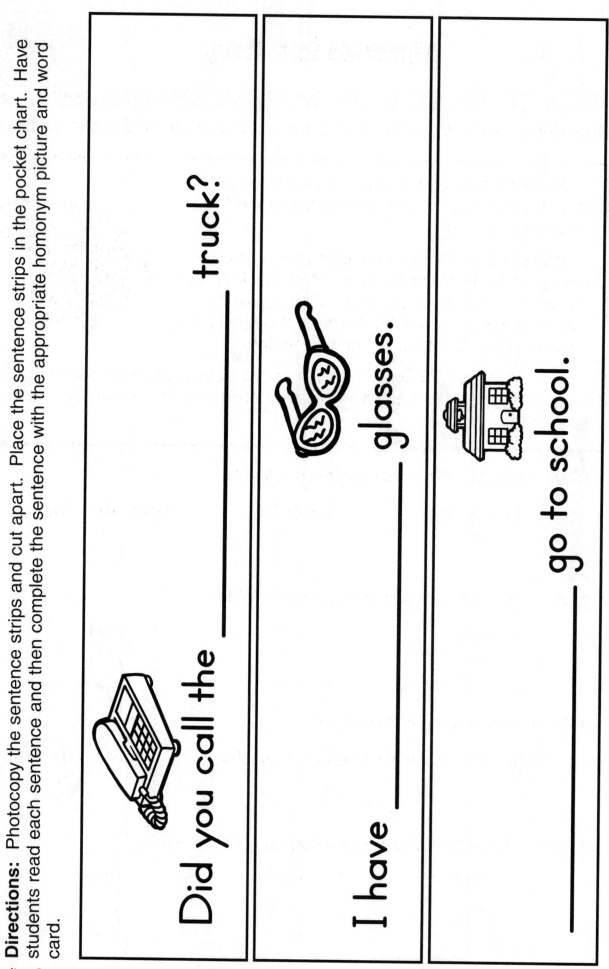

Did you call the _____ truck?

I have _____ glasses.

_____ go to school.

Memorial Day

Directions: Read the information in the box and answer the questions below.

Memorial Day was originally called Decoration Day. It was a day to remember those who died in service to our nation.

On May 5, 1868, General John Logan officially proclaimed it as Memorial Day. Memorial Day was first observed on May 30, 1868. Flowers were placed on the graves of the Union and Confederate soldiers at the Arlington National Cemetery.

In 1873, New York was the first state to officially recognize Memorial Day as a holiday. By 1971, most states were celebrating Memorial Day on the last Monday in May.

1. What was Memorial Day originally called?

Service Day   ◯

Labor Day   ◯

Decoration Day   ◯

2. What year was the first Memorial Day held?

1868   ◯

1873   ◯

1971   ◯

3. Who does Memorial Day honor?

people who died in service to our country   ◯

people who died   ◯

4. When did most states begin recognizing Memorial Day?

1917   ◯

1971   ◯

1873   ◯

May Day

Directions: Read the information in the box and answer the questions below.

May Day is celebrated around the world. May Day is considered the first day of summer. It represents a return to life and new hopes for a good planting and harvest. Traditionally, May Day is celebrated on May 1st.

Since ancient times, May Day has been a day for outdoor festivals. A May Queen was crowned to reign over the games, dancing, and festivities.

A May Pole was made from the trunk of a tall birch tree and decorated with flowers. The May Pole stood for the world center, the hub of the wheel of heaven, or the tree of life. Villagers danced and sang around the May Pole.

1. When is May Day traditionally held?

May 1st ○   May 3rd ○   May 5th ○

2. What season does May Day recognize?

winter ○   summer ○   spring ○

3. What is the May Pole made from?

a birch tree ○   a pine tree ○   a telephone pole ○

4. What do people do with the May Pole?

dance around it ○   read around it ○   sleep around it ○

How Do the Gardens Grow?

Directions: Read each clue. If the answer is "yes," make an **O** in the box. If the answer is "no," make an **X** in the box. Use your answers to solve the questions below.

	Daisies	Roses	Sunflowers	Tulips
Jay				
Jeff				
Nora				
Sara				

CLUES

- Nora grows roses.
- Jeff does not grow sunflowers.
- Jay does not grow tulips.
- Sara does not grow sunflowers or tulips.

1. Jay grows _____.

3. Nora grows _____.

2. Jeff grows _____.

4. Sara grows _____.

Which One Is Mom's Favorite?

Directions: Read the clues. Cross out the pictures that do not fit the clues.

CLUES

- I have two leaves.

- I have more than five petals.

- I have a small center.

Which flower is Mom's favorite?

_____

Directions: Write another clue that would fit the mystery flower.

_____

- -

_____

Who Ate the Plant?

Directions: Read the clues. Cross out the pictures that do not fit the clues.

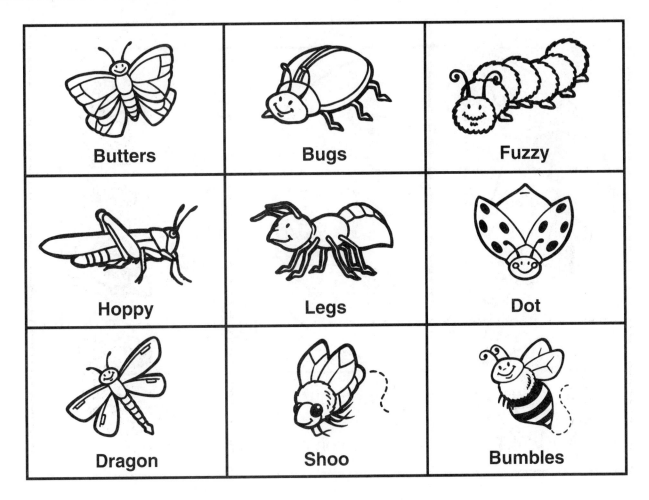

Butters	Bugs	Fuzzy
Hoppy	Legs	Dot
Dragon	Shoo	Bumbles

CLUES

- I have antennas.

- My six legs are showing.

- You can see all three of my body parts.

Which bug am I? _____

Directions: Write another clue that would fit the mystery bug.

_____

- -

_____

Gifts for Mom

Directions: Use the graph to answer the questions.

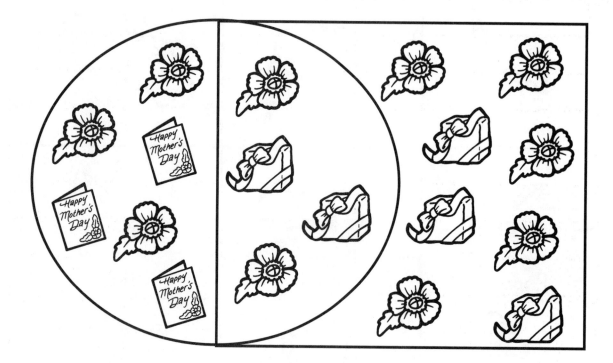

1. How many of each item are shown on the chart?

 _____ _____ _____

2. How many cards are in the square? _____

3. How many flowers are in the circle? _____

4. How many gifts are in the both the square <u>and</u> the circle? _____

5. Which item is in the circle, the square, and in both the circle and the square? _____

6. How many flowers are in <u>only</u> the square? _____

7. How many gifts are in <u>only</u> the circle? _____

Flags Sold

Directions: Use the graph to answer the questions.

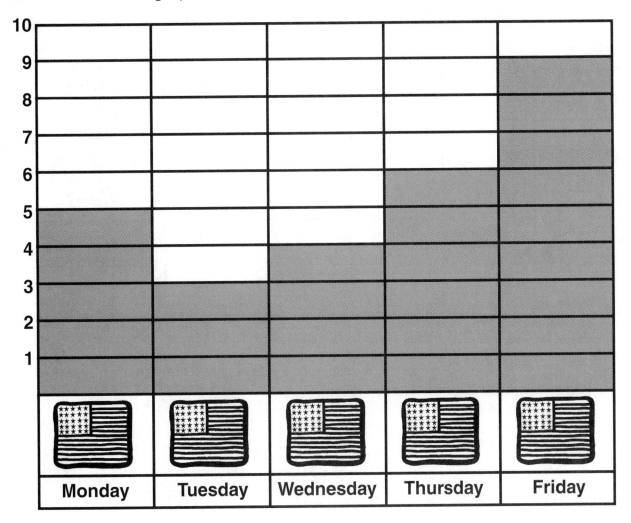

1. On which day were the most flags sold? _____

2. On which day were the fewest flags sold? _____

3. How many flags were sold on Tuesday? _____

4. Were more flags sold on Thursday or Wednesday? _____

5. Were fewer flags sold on Tuesday or Monday? _____

6. How many flags were sold in all? _____

Peanuts

Directions: Ask 10 classmates to name their favorite way to eat peanuts. Use the pictures to create a graph.

Salted						
Butter						
Fudge						

1. Which one did the most kids like the best?

2. Did more kids like ⬡ or 🥫 ?

3. Did more kids like ⬡ or 🥜 ?

4. Which food item do you like the best?

Time #1

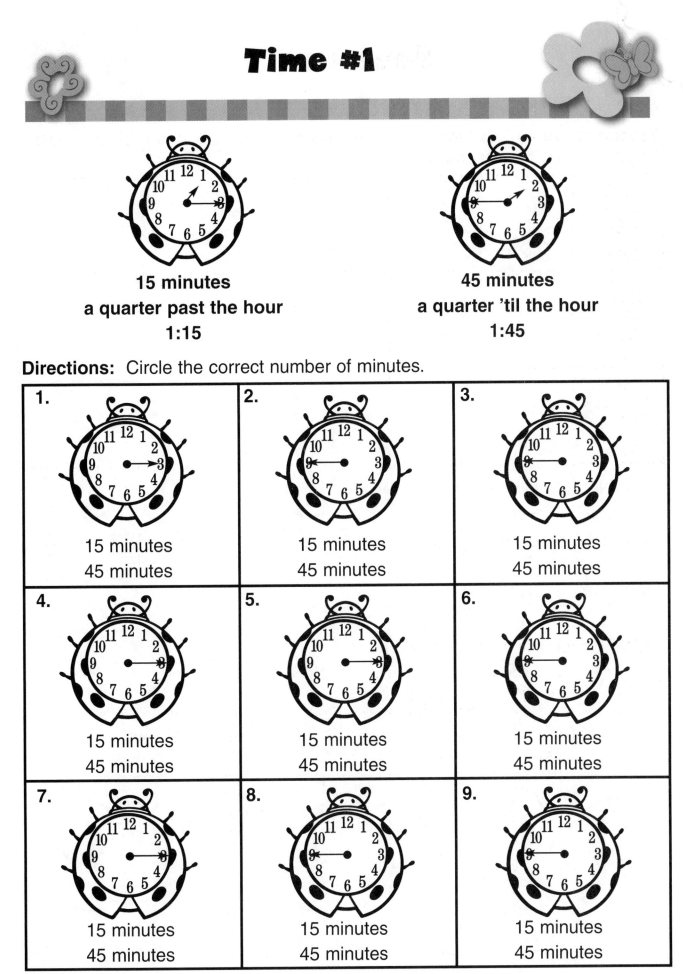

15 minutes
a quarter past the hour
1:15

45 minutes
a quarter 'til the hour
1:45

Directions: Circle the correct number of minutes.

1. 15 minutes 45 minutes	**2.** 15 minutes 45 minutes	**3.** 15 minutes 45 minutes
4. 15 minutes 45 minutes	**5.** 15 minutes 45 minutes	**6.** 15 minutes 45 minutes
7. 15 minutes 45 minutes	**8.** 15 minutes 45 minutes	**9.** 15 minutes 45 minutes

Time #2

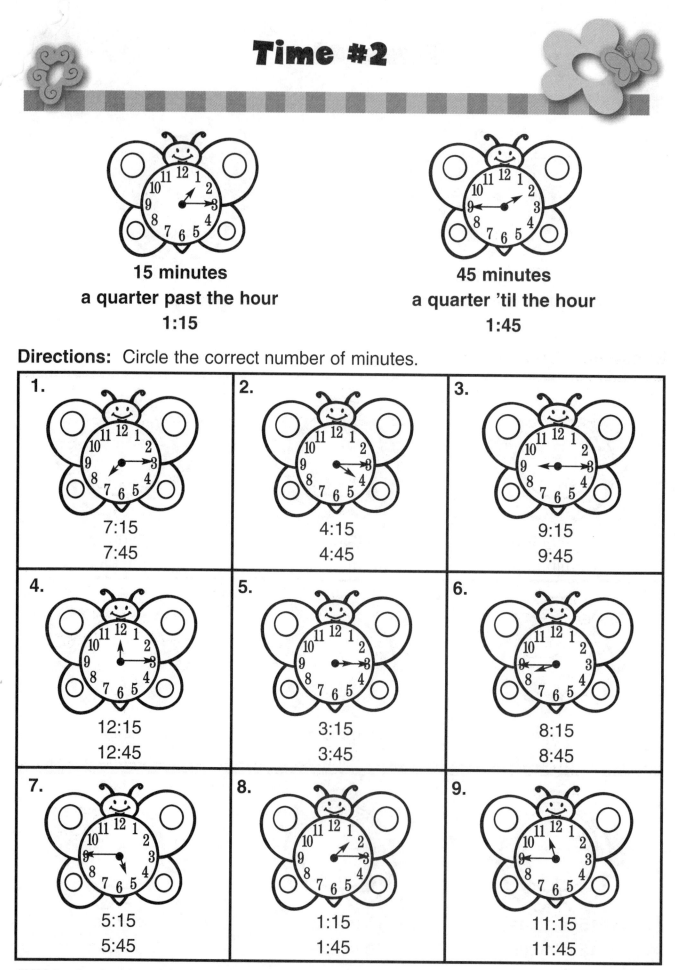

15 minutes
a quarter past the hour
1:15

45 minutes
a quarter 'til the hour
1:45

Directions: Circle the correct number of minutes.

1.
7:15
7:45

2.
4:15
4:45

3.
9:15
9:45

4.
12:15
12:45

5.
3:15
3:45

6.
8:15
8:45

7.
5:15
5:45

8.
1:15
1:45

9.
11:15
11:45

Time #3

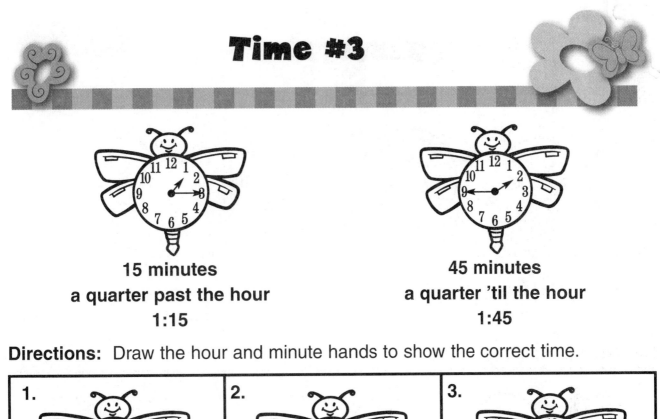

**15 minutes
a quarter past the hour
1:15**

**45 minutes
a quarter 'til the hour
1:45**

Directions: Draw the hour and minute hands to show the correct time.

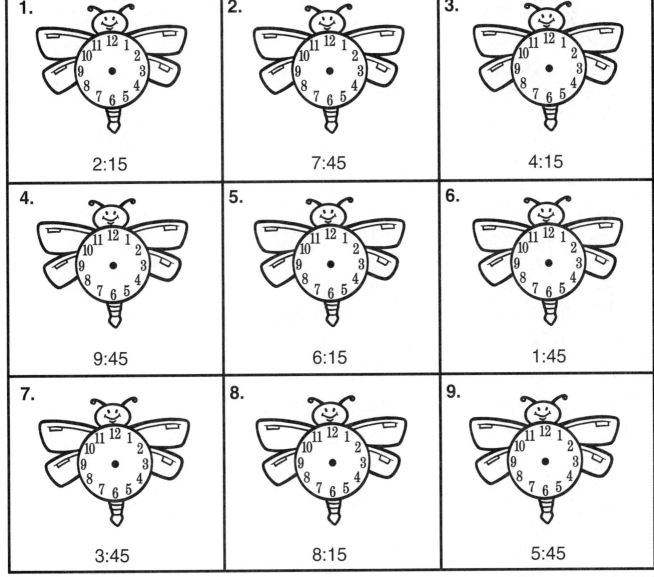

1. 2:15

2. 7:45

3. 4:15

4. 9:45

5. 6:15

6. 1:45

7. 3:45

8. 8:15

9. 5:45

Quarters #1

 quarter
25 cents
25¢

Directions: Count the money. Does it total 25¢? Circle *yes* or *no*.

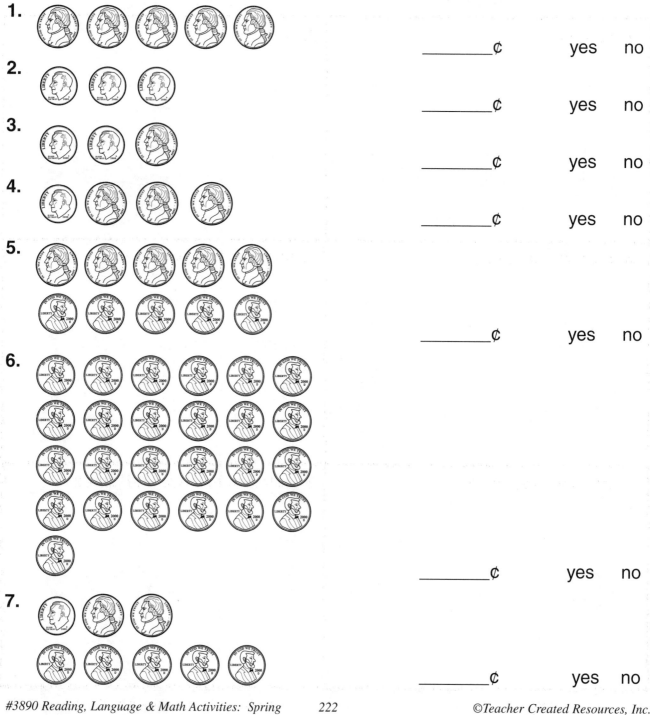

1. _____¢   yes   no

2. _____¢   yes   no

3. _____¢   yes   no

4. _____¢   yes   no

5. _____¢   yes   no

6. _____¢   yes   no

7. _____¢   yes   no

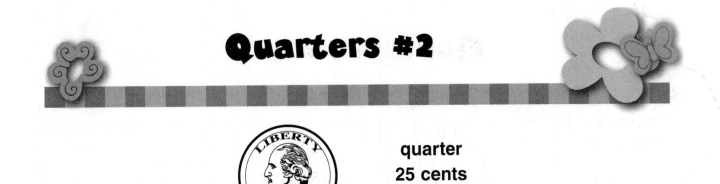

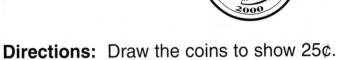

quarter
25 cents
25¢

Directions: Draw the coins to show 25¢.

1. nickels	**2.** pennies
3. nickels and dimes	**4.** pennies and nickels
5. pennies and dimes	**6.** pennies, nickels, and dimes

Plant Power

Directions: Measure the height of each plant to the nearest inch using the ruler at the bottom of the page.

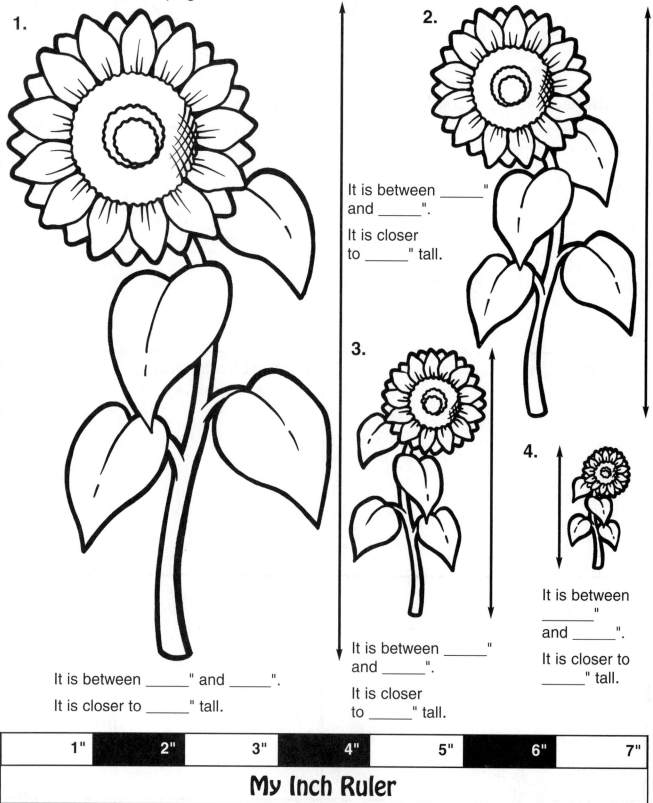

1.

2.

It is between _____"
and _____".

It is closer
to _____" tall.

3.

4.

It is between _____" and _____".

It is closer to _____" tall.

It is between _____"
and _____".

It is closer
to _____" tall.

It is between
_____"
and _____".

It is closer to
_____" tall.

| 1" | 2" | 3" | 4" | 5" | 6" | 7" |

My Inch Ruler

May Calendar

Directions: Photocopy the blank calendar (page 64) and this page. Make a clean copy of the calendar fill-in section first on this page and add any special school or local events in the empty squares. Students' names can be added to the birthday squares. Then photocopy the completed "fill-in" page. Have students add the month and the days of the week to the calendar. Students also can write the current year next to the name of the month. Have students write the calendar numbers in each square. Have students add the special squares to the appropriate dates on the calendar. Using markers or crayons, have students color the calendar. Have students answer questions about the calendar.

(*Optional Step:* Fold a 12" x 18" inch piece of colored construction paper in half which would be 12" x 9". Have students open the folded piece of construction paper and glue or staple the completed calendar to the bottom half of the paper. On the top half, have students draw a picture for the current month.)

Calendar "Fill-Ins"

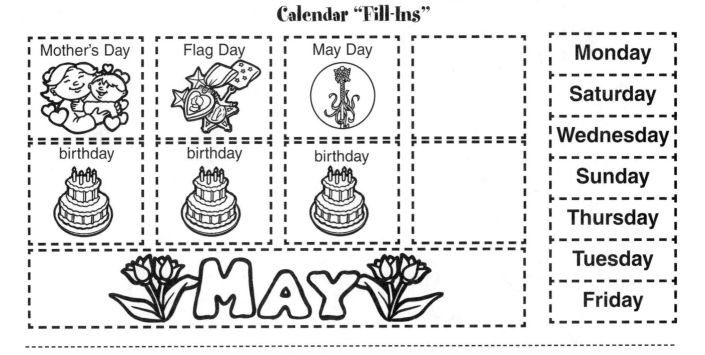

Calendar Questions

1. Mother's Day is the second Sunday in May. What is the date of Mother's Day? _____

2. Memorial Day is the last Monday in May. What is the date of Memorial Day? _____

3. What day of the week is May Day? _____

4. How many school days are in this month? _____

5. On what day does the month end? _____

Remembering

Directions: Cut out the pieces at the bottom of the page. Glue each puzzle piece in the correct space on the graph.

	1	2	3
A			
B			

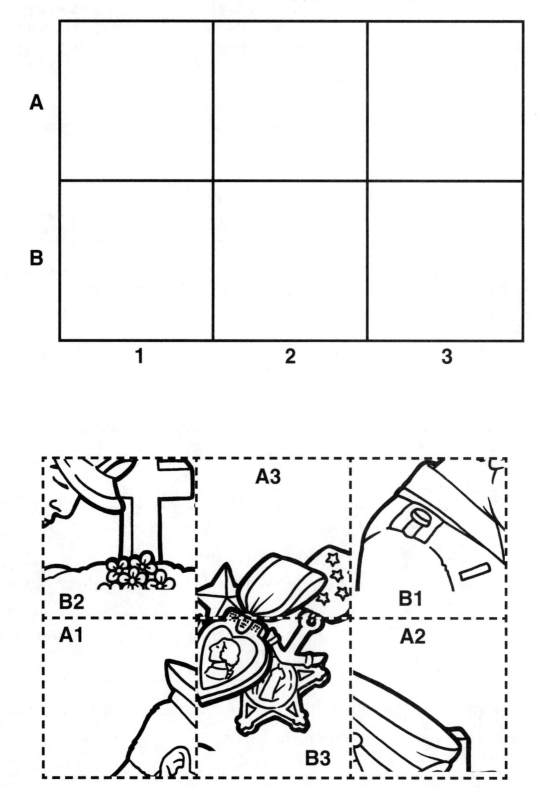

A Butterfly's Life

Directions: Cut out the pieces at the bottom of the page. Glue each puzzle piece in the correct space on the graph.

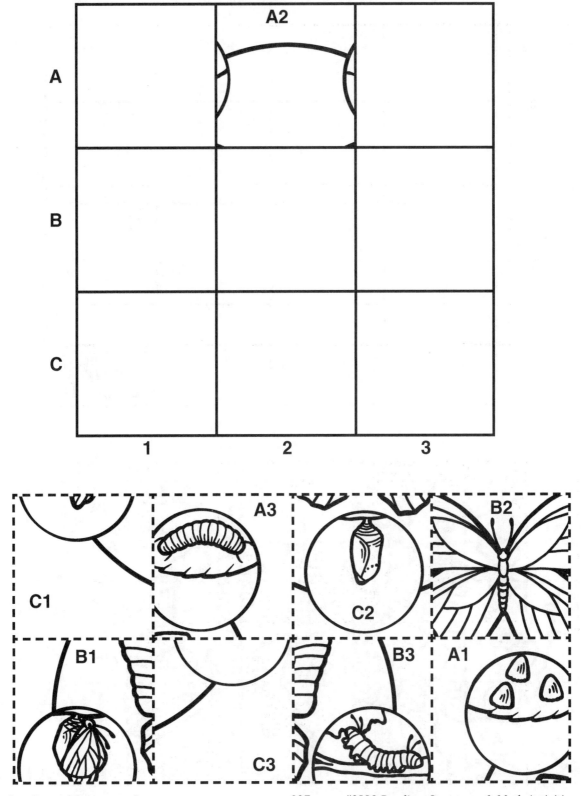

Mom's Day

Directions: Cut out the pieces at the bottom of the page. Glue each puzzle piece in the correct space on the graph.

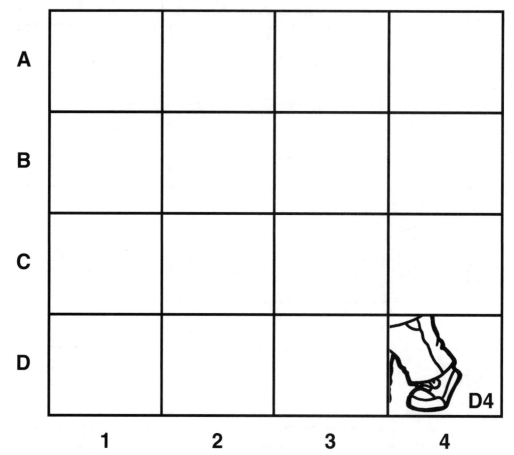

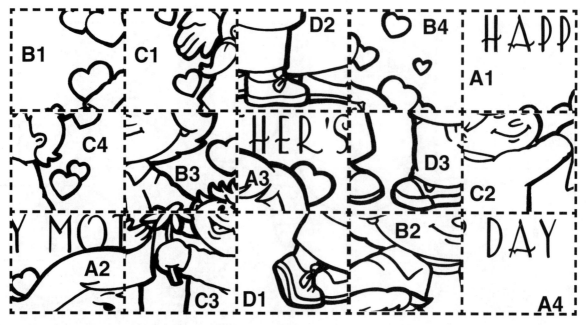

Where's Jack?

Directions: Use the map to answer the questions.

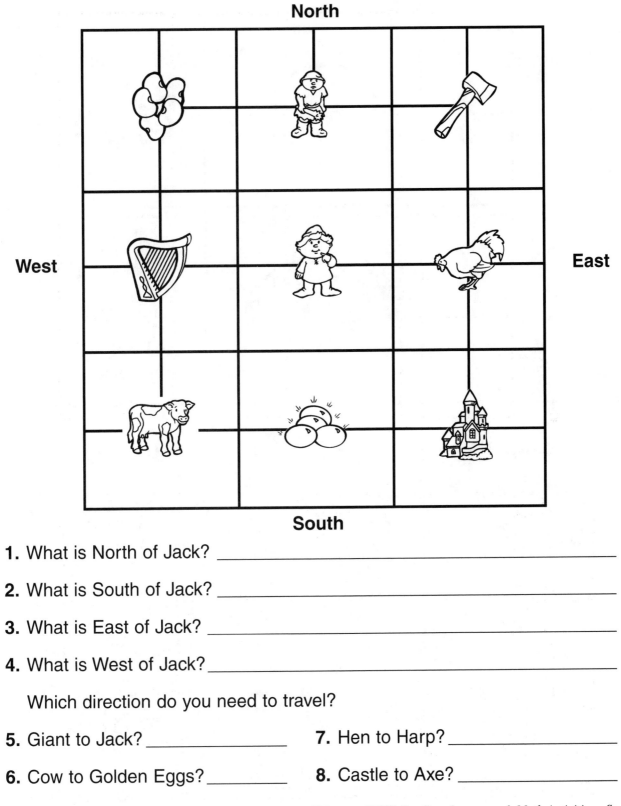

1. What is North of Jack? _____

2. What is South of Jack? _____

3. What is East of Jack? _____

4. What is West of Jack? _____

Which direction do you need to travel?

5. Giant to Jack? _____   7. Hen to Harp? _____

6. Cow to Golden Eggs? _____   8. Castle to Axe? _____

Ladybug Sorting

Directions: Cut out the ladybug pictures. Use the leaf (page 231) to find the different ways the ladybugs can be sorted.

Ladybug Sorting

Directions: Put the ladybugs (page 230) that have something in common onto the leaf.

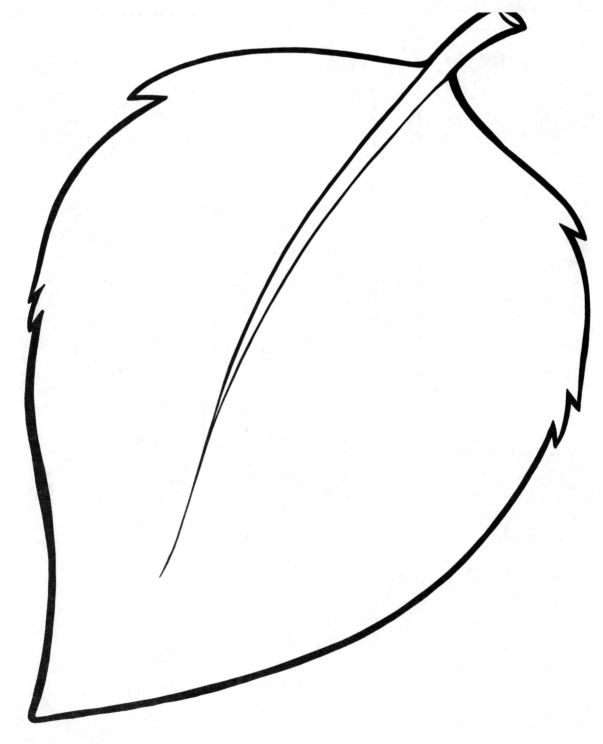

To be in this family _____.

Bug Patterns

Directions: Photocopy a class set of this page onto white construction paper. Have students color and cut out the squares and arrange the squares into different patterns. Glue the squares onto a 12"-long sentence strip.

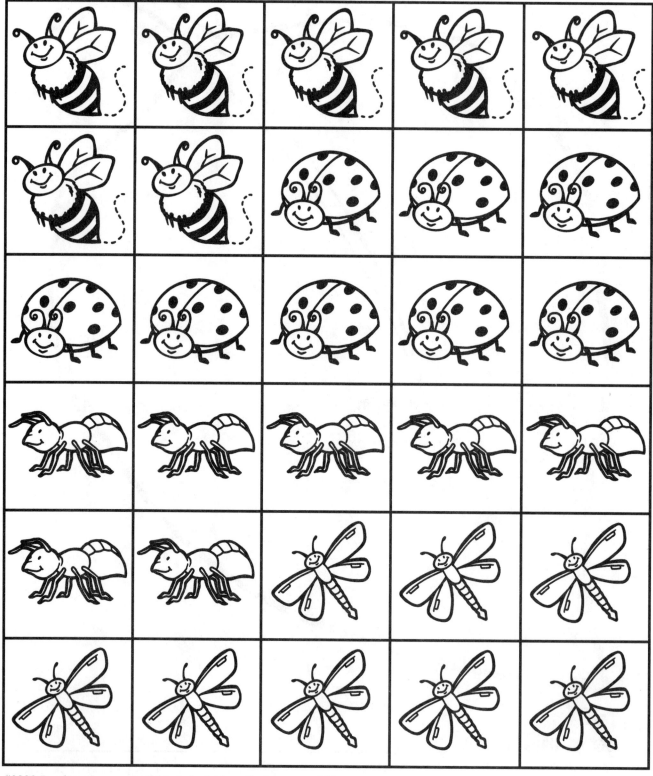

Bug Patterns

Name: _____

Get to the Hive!

This game lets students practice working with place value (tens and ones) and numbers and number word recognition.

Directions

- Photocopy one game board (page 237), one set of game markers (see below), and several sets of place value cards (pages 234–236) for each small group (2–4) of students.

- Each player places his or her game marker in the start box. Taking turns, each player turns over a place value card and moves his/her token to the nearest matching number, number word, or number written in expanded form (using tens and ones).

- If a second player lands in an occupied space, the first player gets bumped back to start.

- The first player to reach the beehive wins the game!

Extension Ideas

- Provide each student with a set of place value cards and a piece of scratch paper. Have the student identify and write the number shown on each place value card.

- Comparing numbers: Provide pairs of students with a couple of sets of the place value cards. Have the students shuffle the cards and divide them evenly between them. Each student turns over his/her top card and compares the two numbers. The student with the larger (or smaller) number wins the round and keeps both cards.

- Sequencing: Put the place value cards in a pocket chart. Have the student sequence the place value cards from smallest to largest.

Game Markers

Get to the Hive!

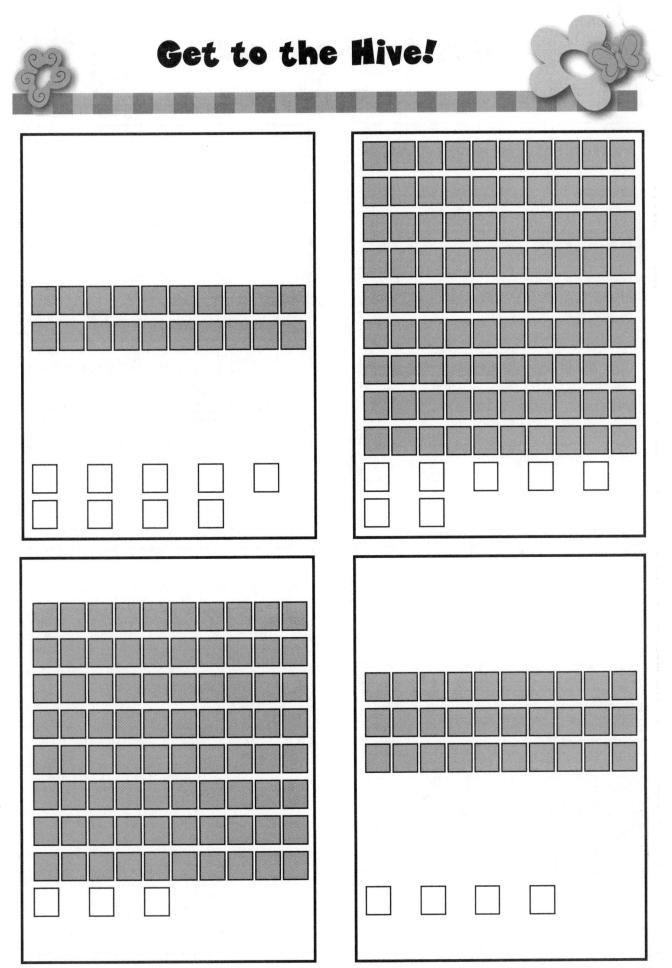

Get to the Hive!

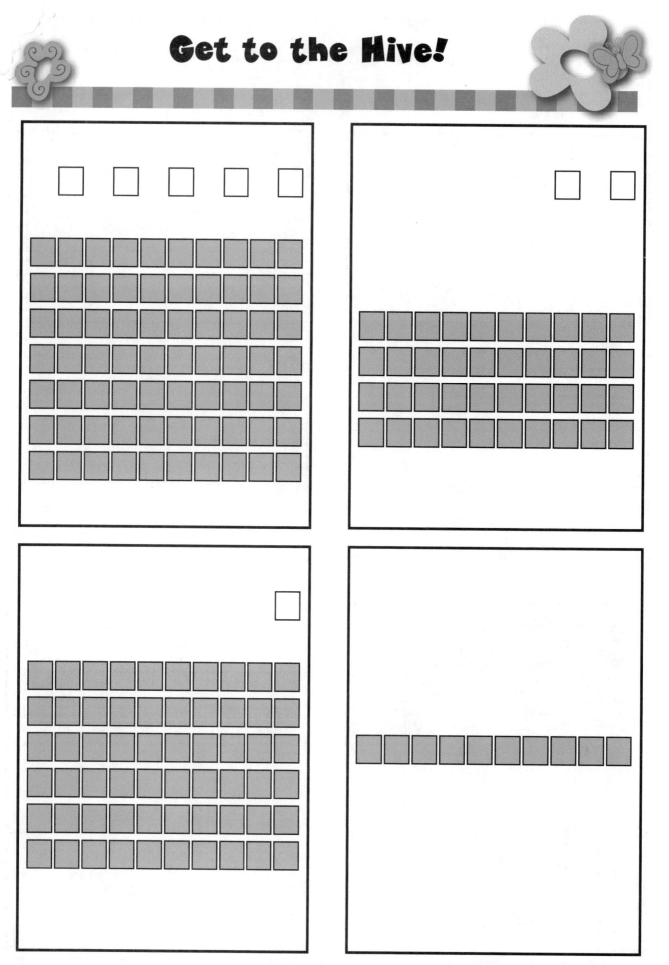

Get to the Hive!

Start

10	seventy-five	80 + 3	4 tens 2 ones	twenty-nine	60 + 1	2 tens 9 ones	34

30 + 4

1 tens 0 ones

6 tens 1 one	90 + 7	3 tens 4 ones	fifty-six	75	40 + 2	eighty-three

20 + 9 · sixty-one

10 = Ten
20 = Twenty
30 = Thirty
40 = Forty
50 = Fifty
60 = Sixty
70 = Seventy
80 = Eighty
90 = Ninety

thirty-four	8 tens 3 ones	10 + 0	56	3 tens 4 ones	eight	forty-two

70 + 5

8	9 tens 7 ones	0 tens 8 ones	ten	5 tens 6 ones

83	7 tens 5 ones	42	50 + 6	ninety-seven	29	61

Answer Key

Page 167

Facts

    Insects have six legs.

    Insects have three body parts.

    Insects can have wings and antennas.

Opinions

    Insects will eat toys.

    Insects are creepy.

    Insects like to scare people

Sample sentence: Insects eat bugs.

Page 168

True Statements

    Plants grow in soil.

    There are many different kinds of plants.

    Plants have stems and roots.

False Statements

    Plants are related to people.

    Plants grow in the sky.

    Plants have bones.

Sample sentence: Plants are good for the environment.

Page 169

1. ant	6. ant
2. butterfly	7. grasshopper
3. dragonfly	8. butterfly
4. grasshopper	9. ladybug
5. ladybug	10. dragonfly

Page 170

1. daisy	6. daisy
2 poinsettia	7. poinsettia
3. rose	8. sunflower
4. sunflower	9. tulip
5. tulip	10. rose

Page 171

1. butter	6. butter
2. caramel	7. milk
3. fudge	8. fudge
4. milk	9. salted
5. salted	10. caramel

Page 175

Page 176

Page 177

Page 178

Page 185

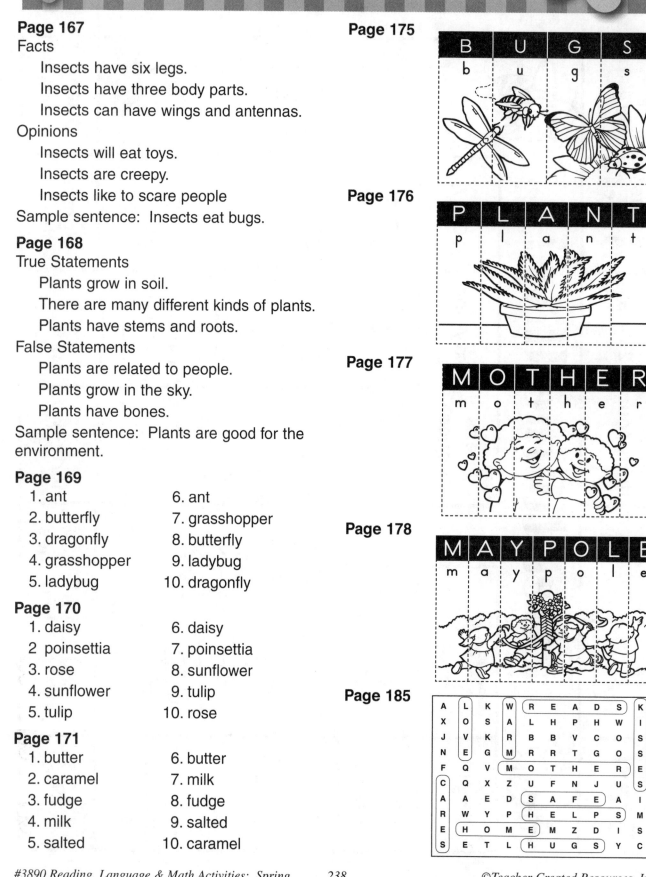

Page 190
1. seeds 3. branch 5. leaf
2. roots 4. trunk 6. sprout

Page 191
1. butterfly 3. bee 5. ant
2. grasshopper 4. dragonfly 6. ladybug

Page 192
1. blossom 3. roots 5. trunk
2. leaf 4. branch

Sample sentence: The rose bush has four blossoms.

Page 193
1. antenna 3. thorax 5. abdomen
2. head 4. leg

Sample sentence: An ant has three body parts.

Page 194
1. Jack sold the cow for five magic beans.
2. The beanstalk grew and grew.
3. Jack climbed the beanstalk.
4. Jack stole the hen that lays golden eggs.
5. The Giant chased Jack down the beanstalk.
6. Jack chopped down the beanstalk.
7. Jack and his mom never went hungry again.

Page 211
1. Decoration Day
2. 1868
3. people who died in service to our country
4. 1971

Page 212
1. May 1st 3. a birch tree
2. summer 4. dance around it

Page 213
1. sunflowers
2. tulips
3. roses
4. daisies

		Daisies	Roses	Sunflowers	Tulips
Jay		X	X	O	X
Jeff		X	X	X	O
Nora		X	O	X	X
Sara		O	X	X	X

Page 214
Number 6
Sample clue: My center is oval-shaped.

Page 215
Legs
Sample clue: I am all one color.

Page 216
1. 10 flowers, 3 cards, 5 gifts
2. 0 5. flower
3. 5 6. 5
4. 2 7. 0

Page 217
1. Friday 4. Thursday
2. Tuesday 5. Tuesday
3. 3 6. 27

Page 218
1. salted 3. salted
2. butter 4. Answers will vary.

Page 219
1 15 minutes 6. 45 minutes
2. 45 minutes 7. 15 minutes
3. 45 minutes 8. 45 minutes
4. 15 minutes 9. 45 minutes
5. 15 minutes

Page 220
1. 7:15 4. 12:15 7. 5:45
2. 4:15 5. 3:15 8. 1:15
3. 9:15 6. 8:45 9. 11:45

Page 221

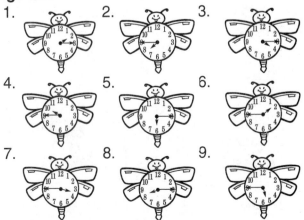

Answer Key

Page 222
1. 25¢, yes
2. 30¢, no
3. 25¢, yes
4. 25¢, yes
5. 30¢, no
6. 25¢, yes
7. 25¢, yes

Page 223
1. Picture should show five nickels.
2. Picture should show 25 pennies.
3. Picture should show three nickels and one dime or one nickel and two dimes.
4. Picture should show four nickels and five pennies or three nickels and 10 pennies or two nickels and 15 pennies or one nickel and 20 pennies.
5. Picture should show two dimes and 5 pennies or one dime and 15 pennies.
6. Picture should show one dime, one nickel, and 10 pennies or one dime, two nickels, and five pennies.

Page 224
1. It is between 6" and 7". It is closer to 7" tall.
2. It is between 4" and 5". It is closer to 4" tall.
3. It is between 2" and 3". It is closer to 3" tall.
4. It is between 1" and 2". It is closer to 1" tall.

Page 226

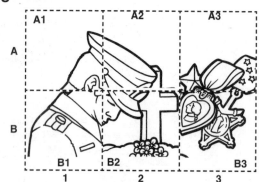

Page 227

Page 228

Page 229
1. giant
2. golden eggs
3. hen
4. singing harp
5. south
6. east
7. west
8. north